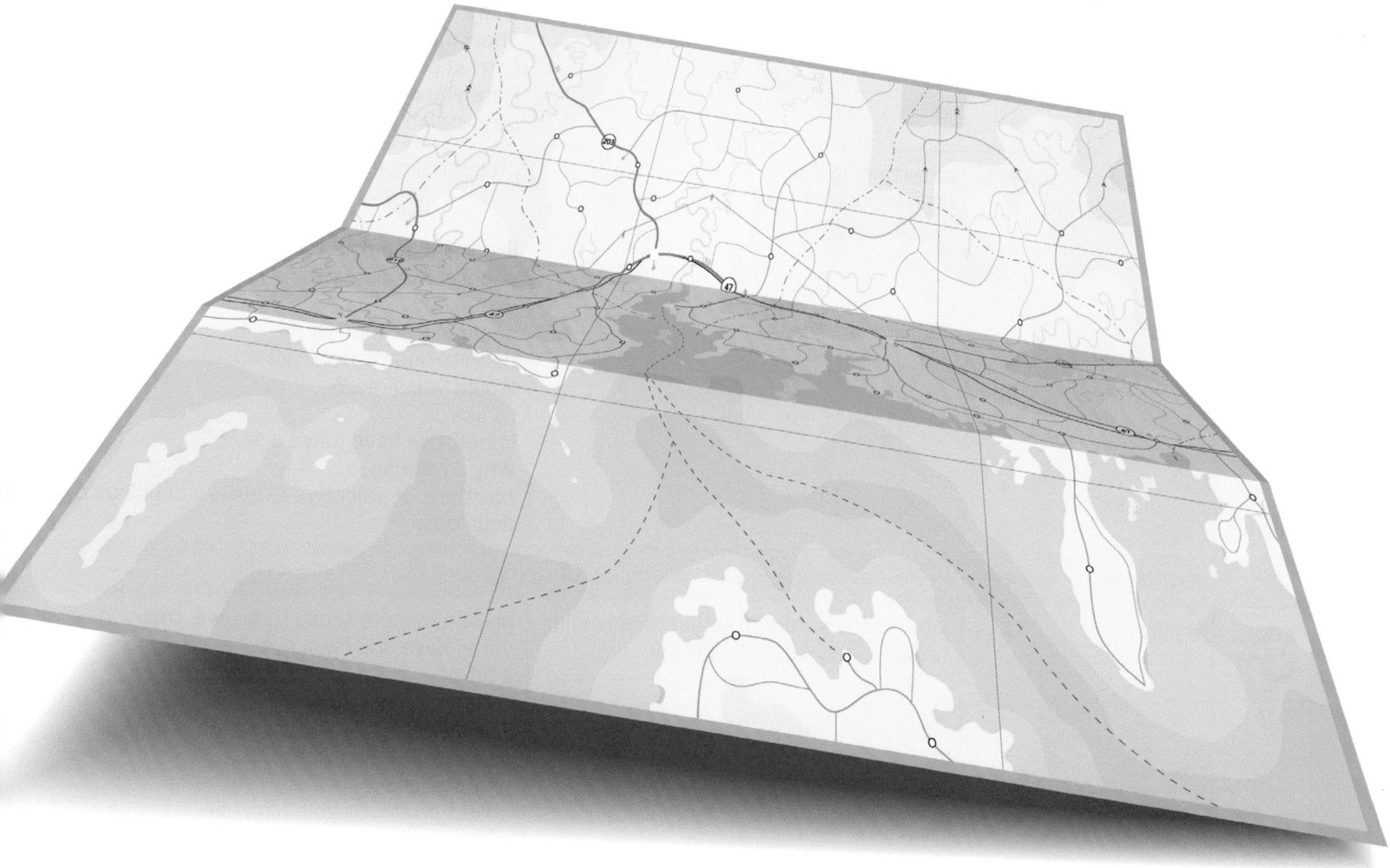

STUDENTS' BOOK 2

NEW ENGLISH PLEASE

RICHARD HARRISON

eBOOK

ALWAYS LEARNING

PEARSON

Contents

Functions	Pronunciation
asking for and giving information/personal details giving addresses describing an office asking to see something	sounds: consonant cluster /dr/ addresses diphthong /əʊ/ show word stress: (two syllable words) sentence stress: (contrastive stress: That's ***my*** computer not ***yours***.)
welcoming visitors offering food and drink accepting/declining offers describing your home describing/asking about likes and dislikes	sounds: consonant /ŋ/ cooking vowel /ɒ/ got diphthongs /əʊ/ goat /aɪ/ like sounds and spelling: ui biscuit, juice gu guest s and sh yes, she ea please, weather strong and weak forms intonation: questions and offers
describing your life (home, jobs, studies, etc.) asking others about home, job, studies etc. giving instructions talking about your children	sounds: vowels /ɜː/ work /ɪ/ sit /ɪː/ seat /eɪ/ get diphthong /eɪ/ gate consonants /p/ peach /b/ beach sounds and spelling: /ɪ/ business, women /f/ photograph word stress: three syllable words
describing and identifying people describing other people's lives, jobs and interests asking about other people's lives buying and selling goods asking the price congratulating	sounds: /r/ price silent r sport, car, far, etc. verb endings /s/ likes /z/ lives /ɪz/ teaches word stress: long words and phrases
describing and asking about daily/weekly routines asking when something happens describing and asking about meals	sounds: consonant cluster /st/ start initial consonants /dʒ/ just /g/ get verb endings /s/ likes /z/ lives diphthong /aʊ/ out vowels /ɪ/ live /ɪː/ leave word stress: two syllable words intonation: questions with When ...?
describing a scene describing present actions ordering food and drink asking where someone is going describing plans asking about and describing the weather	sounds: final /ɪː/ windy initial consonants /p/ place /g/ going /Θ/ thing /ð/ then sounds and spelling: ea steak, head, read /rɪːd/ word stress

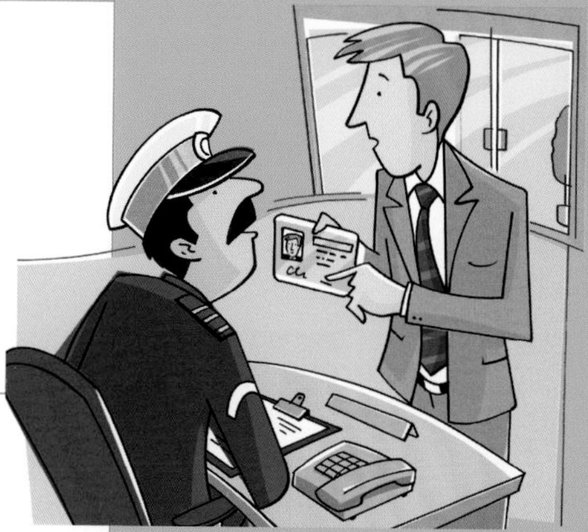

UNIT 1 At work

Lesson 1 A new job

1 **Listen and write**

Write A, B or C.

A Where are you from, Saleem?
I'm from Taif.
Is that near Riyadh?
No, it isn't. It's near Jeddah.

B Have you got a driving licence?
Well, I've got a British driving licence.
Yes, but have you got a Jordanian licence?
No, I haven't.

C Where were you born, Mr Patel?
I was born in Poona.
Poona? Where's that?
It's in India, not far from Mumbai.

Personnel Department

2 **Listen and say**

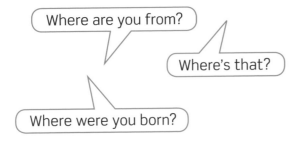

Where are you from?

Where's that?

Where were you born?

LOOK!

Present	Past
I am	I was
You are	You were

I **was** born in Poona.
Where **were** you born?

3 Read

Have you got a ...?

Work Permits (UK)
serving business needs
Work Permits (UK)
Managed Migration
Home Office

work permit

EUROPEAN UNION
UNITED KINGDOM OF
GREAT BRITAIN
AND NORTHERN IRELAND
PASSPORT

passport

VISA

visa

certificate

Diploma

diploma

DVLA
UK

driving licence

4 Ask and answer

A
Have you got a driving licence?

B
Yes, I have.
No, I haven't.

DVLA
UK

EUROPEAN UNION
UNITED KINGDOM OF
GREAT BRITAIN
AND NORTHERN IRELAND
PASSPORT

5 Listen and say

Say the 'dr' sound.
driving licence,
ad**dr**ess, hun**dr**ed,
be**dr**oom, **dr**ink

LANGUAGE

Language
Where were you born?
I was born in ...
Have you got a ... ?
Yes, I have.
No, I haven't.

Lesson 2 What's your address?

1 Listen

Ahmed: What's your address, Mr Robertson?
Jim: My address? It's P.O.Box 50...
Ahmed: P.O.Box 15.
Jim: No. 50 not 15.
Ahmed: Oh, P.O.Box 50.
Jim: Greenwich.
Ahmed: How do you spell that?
Jim: G... R... E... E... N... W... I... C... H.
Ahmed: Greenwich. Yes. And where's that?
Jim: It's a suburb of London.
Ahmed: London. And that's in the United Kingdom?
Jim: Yes.

2 Write

Complete the envelope.

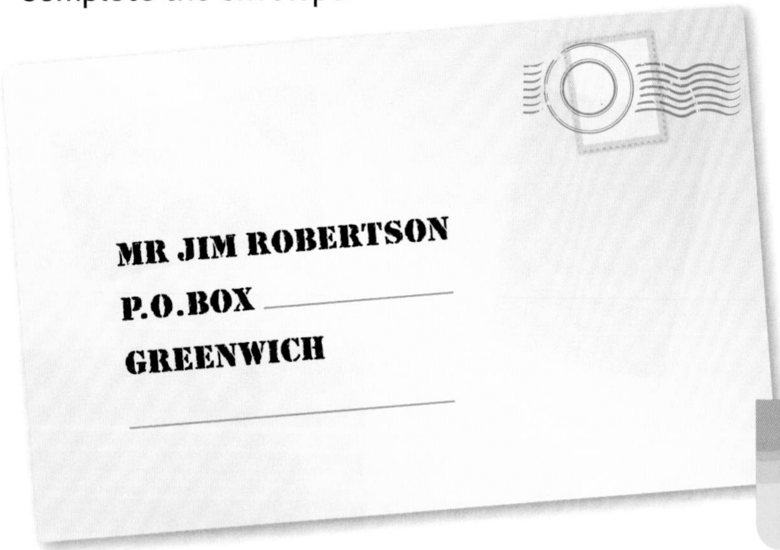
MR JIM ROBERTSON
P.O.BOX ______
GREENWICH
______

LOOK!

P.O.Box = post office box

3 Match

Write the words under the pictures: stamp, letter, address, envelope

Dear Shareholder
Interim dividend payment

______

______

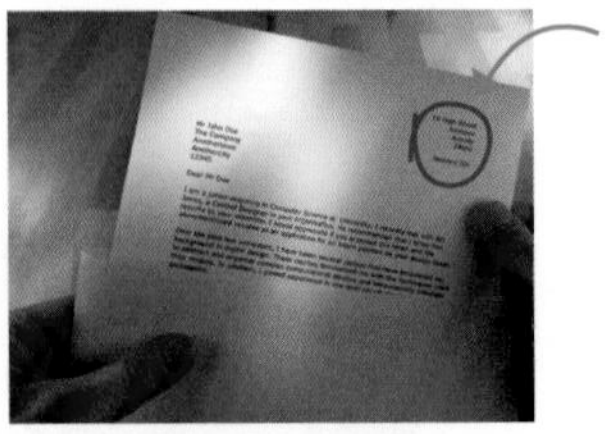

______

1ST

______

4 Listen and say

What's your address?
What's your telephone number?
What's your date of birth?

5 Read

1st, 2nd, 3rd, 4th, 5th, 6th, 7th, 8th, 9th, 10th

6 Listen and say

January, February, March, April, May, June

LOOK!

4th January 2012 = 04/01/12
(the fourth of January, two thousand and twelve)

7 Listen and write

Put the words in the correct list.

morning, today, address, fifteen, suburb, licence, passport, between, hotel, fifty

□ □	□ □
morning	today
______	______
______	______
______	______
______	______

LANGUAGE

What's your address?
My address is ...

Dates
Months: January, February, March, April, May, June

Lesson 3 This is our office

1 Read

Katie has a new job.

This is our office, Katie.
It's nice.
Yes. And this is your desk.
And that's your chair.
And is this my computer?
No. That's Sarah's.
That's yours – over there.
OUT OF ORDER
Oh. I see.

2 Match

Match the words with the pictures:

photocopier, cupboard, chair, desk, computer, shelf, filing cabinet, table

a

____

b

____

c

____

d

____

e

____

f
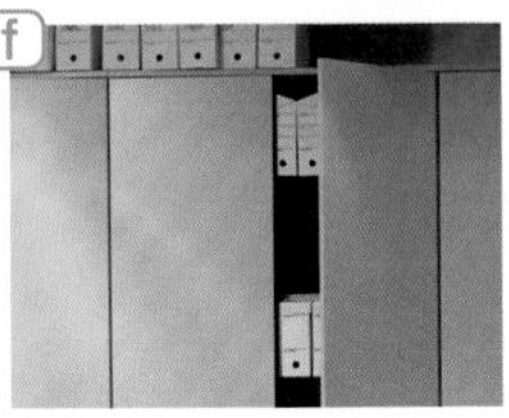
____

g

____

h

____

3 Listen and say

Months: **July, August, September, October, November, December**
Dates: **11th, 12th, 13th, 14th, 15th, 16th, 17th, 18th, 19th, 20th**

4 Match

Write the words under the pictures: **cap**, **hat**, **uniform**, **overalls**

____

____

____

____

5 Write

Write in these words: **next**, **Waleed's**, **over**, **yours**, **where's**, **your**

A: That's (a) ________ locker, Samir.

B: I see. Thanks. And is this my uniform?

A: No, that's (b) ________. This is (c) ________, here.

B: Right. And (d) ________ my cap?

A: It's (e) ________ there, (f) ________ to the door.

6 Listen and say

Sentence stress

a That's **my** computer, not **yours**.
b No. My bag's not **blue**, it's **black**.
c I was born in **March** not **May**.
d She's not from **Jordan**. She's from **Lebanon**.
e My name's **Samira** not **Samir**!

LANGUAGE

Months: July, August, September, October, November, December

Dates: 11th – 20th

Oh good.

I see.

Lesson 4 Show me your pass, please

1 Listen

Guard: Show me your pass, please.
Bob: I'm sorry. I haven't got one.
Guard: Oh! Well, have you got an identification card?
Bob: No I haven't. But I've got a driving licence.
Guard: Can I see it?
Bob: Yes, here you are.
Guard: Thank you. Wait here a minute, please.

2 Write

a Bob hasn't got a ________________.

b He hasn't got an ________________.

c Bob has got a ________________.

3 Ask and answer

A	B
Show me your ..., please.	Yes, here you are.
Can I see your ..., please?	I'm sorry. I haven't got a ....

LOOK!

Show me ... / Can I see ...?

Show me your pass, / passport, / driving licence, please.

Can I see your pass, please?

4 Match

Match the words to the pictures.

NO ENTRY
SLOW
STOP
DANGER
NO SMOKING
NO PARKING

1

2

3
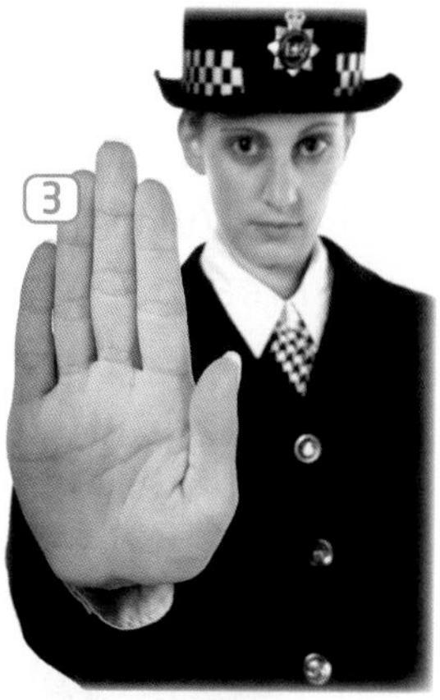

4

5

10
ZONE

6

DANGER OF DEATH
KEEP OUT

5 Read

21st, 22nd, 23rd, 24th, 25th, 26th, 27th, 28th, 29th, 30th, 31st

twenty-first, twenty-second, twenty-third, twenty-fourth, twenty-fifth, twenty-sixth, twenty-seventh, twenty-eighth, twenty-ninth, thirtieth, thirty-first

6 Read the dates

a 1st November 2011

b 12/04/1999

c 26th July 2012

d 3rd Oct.'10

e 21/5/1988

f 21st March 1985

7 Listen and say

Say the '**o**' sound.
Oh!, sh**o**w, sl**o**w, g**o**, n**o**, ph**o**ne, sm**o**king, r**o**ad, d**o**n't, kn**o**w

LANGUAGE

Dates: 21st-31st
Show me ...
Can I see ...?
Here you are.

STUDY

was/were

Present	*Past*
I am	I was
You are	You were
	I **was** born in ...
	Where **were** you born?

Have you got a ...?	Yes, I have.
	No, I haven't.

my/mine

It's	my ...	mine
	your ...	yours
	his ...	his
	her ...	hers
	our ...	ours
	your ...	yours
	their ...	theirs

'Is this **my** desk?'	'No, that's **mine**. That's **yours** over there.'
'Is that **her** filing cabinet?'	'No, it isn't **hers**. It's **ours**.'
'Is that **Salwa's** computer?'	'No, this is **Salwa's**, here.'

Show me ..., please.
Can I see ..., please?
Yes. Here you are.

Dates

31/10/2003	= 31st Oct. 2003	= the thirty-first of October, two thousand and three
23/04/94	= 23rd April 1994	= the twenty-third of April, nineteen ninety-four
02/01/2010	= 2nd Jan. 2010	= the second of January, two thousand and ten

What's your address?
telephone number?
date of birth?

NEW WORDS

Learn these words.

Office vocabulary
filing cabinet
typewriter
address
envelope
stamp
shelf/shelves
computer

Countries
India
United Kingdom
Pakistan

Nationalities
Indian
Jordanian
British

Months
January
February
March
April
May
June
July
August
September
October
November
December

Clothes
hat
cap
overalls
uniform

Verbs
wait
show

Documents
pass
work permit
document
certificate
diploma
identification card
driving licence

Others
suburb
district
date of birth
main gate
guard
slow
at work

Write other new words here.

UNIT
2 At home

Lesson 1 Please come in

1 **Listen and read**

It's Monday afternoon. Liz has a visitor.

Please come in.
Thank you.

Have a seat, Ann.
Thanks.

Would you like some tea?
Yes, please.
Sugar?
No, thanks.

Have a biscuit.
Thanks.

Mmmm. They're delicious!

2 **Match**

Write the words under the pictures:
coffee, **sugar**, **tea**, **a sandwich**, **a cake**

__________ __________ __________ __________ __________

3 Listen and say

Would you like some tea?
Would you like a biscuit?
Have a sandwich.

LOOK!

Saying 'Yes': **Yes**, please.
Thank you.
Saying 'No': **No**, thank you.
No, thanks.

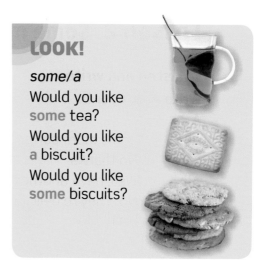

LOOK!

some/a
Would you like **some** tea?
Would you like **a** biscuit?
Would you like **some** biscuits?

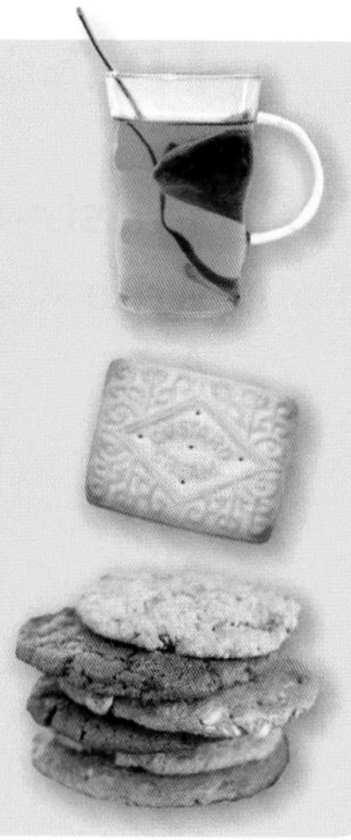

4 Ask and answer

A

Would you like a/some ...?

Have a/some ...

B

Yes, please.

No, thank you.

No, thanks.

Have a biscuit.
Thanks.

5 Listen and say

Sounds and spelling.
'**sss**' and '**sh**'
sss: **s**peak, **s**ay, **s**it down, ye**s**, poli**ce**, ni**ce**, **c**ity, pala**ce**
sh: **s**ugar, **sh**e, pu**sh**, **sh**op, na**ti**onality, deli**c**ious, mousta**che**

6 Listen and say

Listen and say the weak forms of these words:
a some, a, of, you, to, for
b some tea, a cup of tea, would you like, to Mary, it's for you
c Would you like some tea?
Can I speak to Mary?

7 Listen

Sounds and spelling
Biscuit, building, juice, suitcase

LANGUAGE

Would you like ...?
Have a ... .
some/a some tea, a biscuit
Yes, please.
No, thank you.
It's delicious. They're delicious.
at home

Lesson 2 Some more coffee

1 Listen and write

Write A, B, C, or D.

A

Ali: Some more coffee, Sam?
Sam: No thanks.
Ali: Well, have another cake.
Sam: No. They're delicious, but I'm full.

B

Liz: Would you like some fruit?
Ann: Yes, I would.
Liz: Help yourself.
Ann: Thanks. I think I'll have an apple.

C

Nadia: How's the coffee?
Tom: It's fine thanks.
Mary: Can I have some milk please?
Nadia: Of course. Here you are.
Mary: Thanks. That's enough.

D

Hassan: Have some more meat.
Jim: Yes. I'd like some more.
Hassan: And would you like some more salad?
Jim: No thanks. I've got enough.

2 Match

Match the words to the pictures: **meat, rice, salad, bread, chicken**

3 Ask and answer

Offer your guest

some more: rice, meat, bread, salad, ice-cream, chicken

or **another**: cake, biscuit, apple, orange, cup of coffee, sandwich

LOOK!

would

Would you like some fruit?

Yes. I'd like an orange.

I'd = I would

I **would** like an orange.

Would you like an orange? Yes, I would.

4 Look and say

What would these people like?

Make sentences with: I'd like ….

5 Write

Write in these words:

I'd, **full**, **another**, **some**, **here**, **of course**, **thanks**, **have**, **down**, **would**

Mike: Please sit (a) ____________, Jameel.

Jameel: Thanks.

Mike: Would you like (b) ____________ orange juice.

Jameel: Yes, I (c) ____________. I'm very thirsty.

Mike: (d) ____________ you are.

Jameel: Thanks.

Fatima: (e) ____________ some dates, Mary. They're sweet.

Mary: No (f) ____________.

Fatima: Or would you like (g) ____________ cake?

Mary: No, really. I'm quite (h) ____________. But (i) ____________ like a glass of water.

Fatima: (j) ____________. Just a minute.

LOOK!

a	glass	of	water
	cup		tea
	can		cola

6 Listen and say

Say the "**I**" sound.

I, **I'd**, **like**, **my**, **mine**, **ice-cream**, **five**, **Irish**, **good-bye**, **time**, **dining room**

LANGUAGE

some more
another
I'd/would
I'd like ….
Here you are.
Help yourself.

Lesson 3 I like hot weather

1 Listen

Bashir: Come in, Peter.
Peter: Thanks.
Bashir: This is my brother, Waleed.
Peter: How do you do?
Waleed: Pleased to meet you.
Bashir: Have a seat. Would you like a cold drink, Peter? There's cola, orange ...
Peter: Have you got any lemonade?
Bashir: Lemonade? Yes. Here you are.
Peter: Thanks. That's good. Isn't it hot today?
Waleed: Yes, very. But I like hot weather.
Peter: Do you? I don't. I like cold weather. I like Bahrain in the winter.
Bashir: Me too. Have some more lemonade, Peter.
Peter: Thanks.

LOOK!

Like
I **like** cold weather.
I **don't like** hot weather.
Do you like hot weather?
don't = do not
I don't speak French.
I do not speak French.

Cola

Which is Peter's drink?

2 Write

Write sentences with *don't*.

a I like football very much. (table-tennis)

____

b I know her name. (address)

____

c I understand French. (German)

____

d I have a job. (a house)

____

e I speak English very well. (Urdu)

____

3 Look and say

I like ... (very much)   I don't like ...

4 Ask and answer

Now ask another student about the pictures above.

A: Do you like ...?

B: No, I don't.

> **LOOK!**
>
> **some/any**
> Have you got **any** lemonade?
> I haven't got **any** petrol.
> I haven't got **any** biscuits.
> I've got **some** water.
> I've got **some** cakes.

5 Listen and say

Say the '**O**' sound

Oh!, n**o**, d**o**n't g**o**, c**o**ld, s**o**, bel**o**w

Say the 'o' sound:

h**o**t, g**o**t, n**o**t, j**o**b, st**o**p, w**a**tch, cl**o**ck

6 Listen and tick (✓)

a	☐ got	☐ goat
b	☐ got	☐ goat
c	☐ got	☐ goat
d	☐ got	☐ goat
e	☐ not	☐ note
f	☐ not	☐ note
g	☐ not	☐ note
h	☐ not	☐ note

10
10 EURO

7 Listen and say

Sounds and spelling.

r**ea**d, pl**ea**se, t**ea**cher, r**ea**lly,
n**ea**r, w**ea**ther, br**ea**d, h**ea**d

> **LANGUAGE**
>
> I like ... .
> I don't like ... (+ a noun)
> Do you like ... ?
> some/any
> in the winter, in the summer

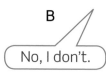

Lesson 4 I like cooking

1 Listen

Sarah: Do you like cooking, Lina?
Lina: Yes, I do. I like it very much. Do you?
Sarah: No. Not much.
Lina: Why not?
Sarah: Because it's difficult.
Lina: Difficult? No, it isn't. It's easy. I'll teach you.
Sarah: OK.
Lina: Look. This is 'foul medames'.
Sarah: What?
Lina: 'Foul medames'. It's an Egyptian dish.
Sarah: What is it in English?
Lina: I'm not sure. Beans, I think.
Sarah: Hmmm. I like beans.
Lina: Good. Well, the first thing is ...

a What is foul medames in English?
b Where is foul medames from?

LOOK!

I **like** cooking.
I **don't like** cooking.
Do you **like** cooking? Yes, I do.
No, I don't.

2 Listen and say

Do you like: cooking?
reading?
driving?
learning English?
watching television?

LOOK!

-ing
I like cook**ing**.
read**ing**.
learn**ing** English.
driv**ing**.

VERB	+	-ING		
cook	+	-ing	=	cooking
read	+	-ing	=	reading
learn	+	-ing	=	learning
drive	+	-ing	=	driving

3 Ask and answer

Ask another student.

A

Do you like ... (cooking)?

B

Yes, I do.
No, I don't.
Yes, I like ... very much.
No. Not much.

4 Match

Write these words under the pictures:

walking, **reading**, **swimming**, **watching TV**, **learning English**, **driving**, **fishing**, **cooking**, **shopping**

a ____________ b ____________ c ____________ d ____________ e ____________

f ____________ g ____________ h ____________ i ____________

5 Match

It's ... **difficult**/**easy**/**interesting**.

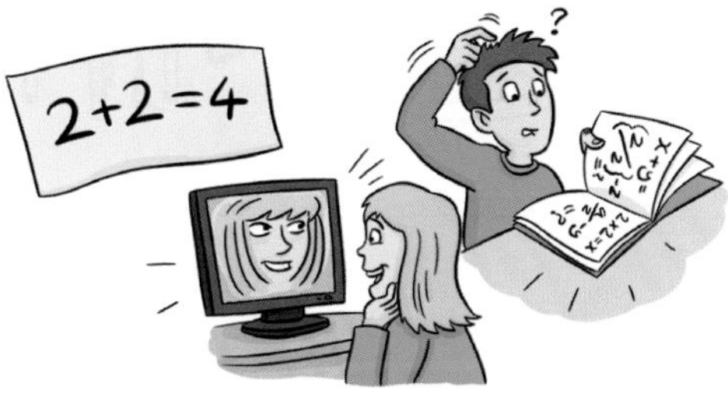
2+2=4

6 Write

Write these words:

much, **very**, **don't**, **interesting**, **because**, **do**, **driving**, **too**, **why**, **like**

A: (a) ____________ you like (b) ____________, Martin?

B: No. Not (c) ____________.

A: Why not?

B: (d) ____________ there are a lot of cars on the road.

C: I (e) ____________ reading very much.

D: Me (f) ____________. It's very (g) ____________.

C: But I (h) ____________ like watching television.

D: (i) ____________ not?

C: Because the programmes aren't (j) ____________ good.

LOOK!

Why ...? Because ...

Why don't you like cooking, Sarah?

Because it's difficult.

LANGUAGE

+ ing (cooking, learning, going)

I like ... (+ -ing)

I don't like ... (+ -ing)

Do you like ...? (+ -ing)

Why?

Because ...

difficult/easy

very much

not much

STUDY

The Present Simple Tense

I like ...	Do you like ...?	I don't speak English.
I don't like ...	I speak English.	Do you speak English?

-ing forms Verb + -ing

cook + -ing = cooking

I like cooking. I don't like driving. Do you like playing basketball?

Would

Would you like ...? Yes, I would. I'd like ...

Have ...

Have a seat. some fruit. another cup of coffee.

come in go out sit down stand up

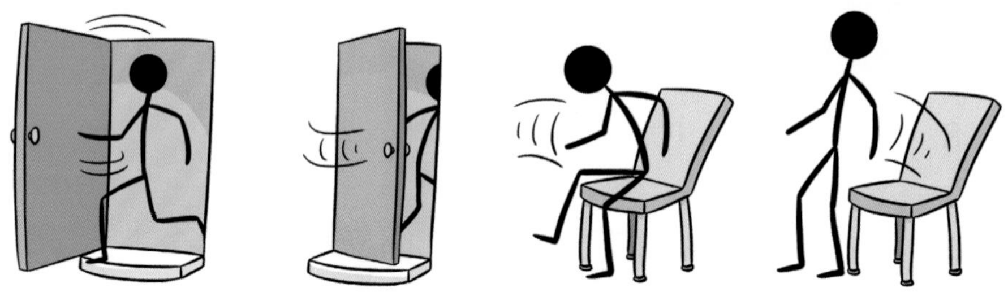

Saying 'Yes':
Yes, please.
Thank you.

Saying 'No':
No, thanks.
No, thank you.

Countable/Uncountable nouns

Uncountable nouns: water, tea, rice, bread, milk

I'd like some tea.

I'd like some more tea.

Countable nouns: biscuit, cake, date, apple

I'd like a biscuit.

I'd like some biscuits.

I'd like another biscuit.

I'd like some more biscuits.

Some/any

I've got some nice biscuits. I haven't got any bread.

Have you got any milk?

Why do you like cooking? Because it's interesting.

Why ...? Because ...

NEW WORDS

Learn these words.

Food
chicken
meat
beans
bread
sugar
cake
biscuit

verbs (-ing)
cooking
driving
walking
swimming
watching
learning
playing
visiting
fishing
shopping

Drink
lemonade
milk
cola
water
(a) drink

Verb
to like

Adjectives
interesting
easy
difficult
delicious

Other
summer
winter
weather
glass
can
cup
dish
goat
note
at home
help yourself
enough
the first thing

Write other new words here.

Revision A

Grammar

1 Write

Present	Past
I am	I was
you are	you were

Write **am ('m)**, **are**, **was** or **were** in the spaces.

A: Where (a) ________ you from, Tariq?

B: I (b) ________ from Lahore in Pakistan.

A: (c) ________ you born in Pakistan?

B: No. I (d) ________ born in Delhi in India.

A: So what's your nationality? (e) ________ you Indian?

B: No. I (f) ________ Pakistani.

2 Write

Countable	a biscuit an orange	some biscuits some oranges
Uncountable	some tea some sugar	

Write **a**, **an** or **some** in the spaces.

Have ________ dates.
I think I'll have ________ banana.
Would you like ________ coffee?
________ more rice?
I'd like ________ apple, please.
Have ________ seat.
I'd like ________ umbrella.

A

3 Question words

Write in the question words: **Who? Whose? Where? What? Why? How? How much? How old?**

a ______ is that bag? — I think it's Sam's.

b ______ is Fawzia? — She's in the sitting room.

c ______ is the cake? — It's delicious.

d ______ is your son? — He's six months.

e ______ do you like that book? — Because it's interesting.

f ______ 's your address? — P.O.Box 432, Jubail, Saudi Arabia.

g ______ is that car? — Five thousand dollars.

h ______ is that? — That's my uncle Nigel.

4 Write

The Present Simple Tense

I like ...

I don't like ...	Yes, I do.
Do you like ...?	No, I don't.

LOOK!

have and have got

I **have** two children.
I **have got** two children.
I **don't have** any children.
I **haven't got** any children.
Do you have any children?
Have you got any children?

Make sentences with don't. For example:

I like Cairo in the winter. (summer)
I don't like Cairo in the summer.

a I speak French very well. (English)

____

b I like my house very much. (my job)

____

c I know their daughter's name. (their son's name)

____

d I have three brothers. (any sisters)

____

Make questions with Do you ...? For example:

like/music?	Do you like music?
e like/your job?	______________
f speak/Arabic?	______________
g know/my village?	______________
h have/a car?	______________

5 Ask and answer

Dates.
20/05/95 = 20th May 1995
What's the date?
It's the twentieth of May nineteen ninety-five.

Ask your partner: **What's the date? It's the ...**

a 2nd Jan. 2006
b 25/09/08
c 31st Oct. '89
d 03/12/94
e 14th Aug. 2001
f 25th Apr. '08
g 23/06/97
h 20/11/09
i 17th Sept. 2010
j 22/05/99

What's today's date? It's the ______________

____

New Words

6 Months of the year

What are these months?

a ___ly
b D_c__b__
c M_rc_
d S_pt_m__r
e _pr__
f _a_
g J__e
h _an__ry
i _ov___er
j F__ru__y
k __t_b__
l A_g___

Now write them in order.

January ____

____

7 In the office

Match the words with the pictures: **filing cabinet**, **shelves**, **photocopier**, **stamp**, **envelope**, **address**, **computer**

a
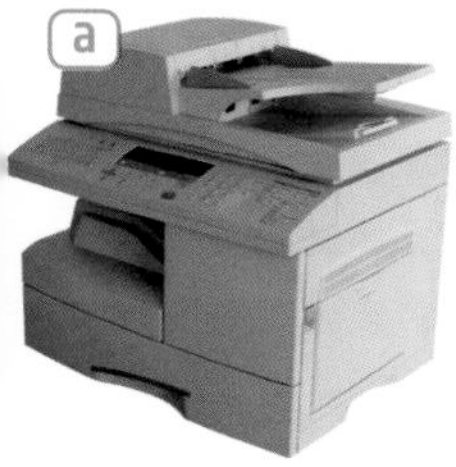

b

c

d
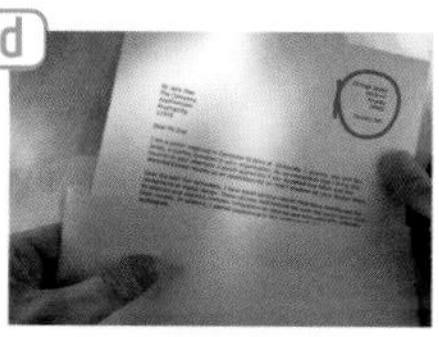

e

f

g

8 Food and drink

Find and circle six things to eat and six things to drink. Write the words.

X	R	T	E	A	J	L	S
B	R	J	U	I	C	E	A
I	Z	H	F	Y	B	M	L
S	T	R	O	M	R	O	A
C	H	I	C	K	E	N	D
U	B	C	F	Q	A	A	X
I	M	E	A	T	D	D	O
T	I	V	W	A	T	E	R
Q	L	G	P	I	C	H	E
A	K	C	O	F	F	E	E

1 ________ 7 ________
2 ________ 8 ________
3 ________ 9 ________
4 ________ 10 ________
5 ________ 11 ________
6 ________ 12 ________

9 Write

verb	+	-ing	
cook		–ing	= cooking
read		–ing	= reading

Write sentences about the pictures.

For example:
I like cooking.
I don't like reading.

a ______________________ e ______________________

b ______________________ f ______________________

c ______________________ g ______________________

d ______________________ h ______________________

Punctuation

10 Write

Put in the punctuation and the capital letters.

a would you like some more salad ______________________

b whats your date of birth ______________________

c i was born in baghdad in iraq ______________________

d have you got a driving licence ______________________

e i don't like learning English ______________________

f mr m h ali ______________________

p o box 234 ______________________

damascus ______________________

syria ______________________

Spelling

11 Look

Find two mistakes in each line.

a *cooking, driveing, playing, reading, waching*

b *bread, cake, meat, slad, sandewich, rice*

c *permit, dibloma, pass, document, cartificat*

d *streat, district, city, country, campany, name*

e *guest, gard, garage, goal, galass, green*

f STOP, DANGRE, VISITORS, NO SMOKKING, SLOW, NO PARKING

Pronunciation

12 Match

Match the words that have the same sounds.

show Oh! time got head juice please would

bye don't cold too watch good bread see

13 Match

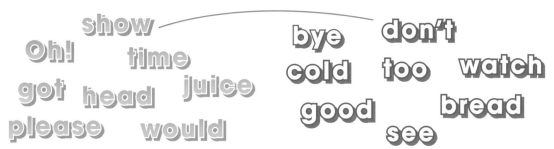

Match the questions with the answers to make a dialogue.

a Some more juice?
b Here you are.
c Would you like a cold drink?
d No, I haven't. But I've got some orange juice.
e Have some dates.

A: ______________________________
B: Yes, I would. Have you got any lemonade?

A: ______________________________
B: Orange juice is fine.

A: ______________________________
B: Thank you.

A: ______________________________
B: Yes, please. Hmmm. They're very sweet.

A: ______________________________
B: No, thanks. That's enough.

Read and Write

14 Read

Read about these people:

My name's Carol. I'm a teacher and I'm from London in England. I'm married and I have two children. I like playing sports, but I don't like swimming. I also like learning languages and at the weekend I like visiting my friends and relatives in London. I have a car, but I don't like driving. The roads are very busy!

I'm Gamal. I'm from Alexandria in Egypt. I'm a taxi driver and I like driving. In the evening I like watching television or reading a book. I don't like playing sports, but I like watching them on television. I have a wife and six children. I speak some English but I don't like learning languages. I'm not a good student.

My name is Waleed. I am an engineer in a big oil company in Yemen. I am single. I like playing sports very much and I also like fishing and swimming. I don't like reading and I don't like watching television, because I think they are boring. I don't like visiting relatives, because I don't have enough time. I have a very busy life.

I'm Suhair and I come from Sharjah in the United Arab Emirates. I'm a secretary in a small insurance company. I'm married, but I don't have any children. I like shopping, reading and learning languages. I speak English and Farsi quite well and I understand a little Urdu. I don't like watching television very much in the evening. I like visiting my sisters and my parents.

Who are they? Write the names: **Carol**, **Gamal**, **Waleed**, **Suhair**

NAME	visiting relatives	driving	playing sports	watching TV	reading	learning languages
a ________	✗		✓	✗	✗	
b ________	✓			✗	✓	✓
c ________		✓	✗	✓	✓	✗
d ________	✓	✗	✓			

15 Write

Read about Carol, Gamal, Waleed, and Suhair again. Now write a paragraph about your life. What's your name? Where are you from? What's your job? What do you like doing?

Story: Hello London 4

Ali and his grandfather are in London.

1
Where's New Street?
Show me the address, please.
2
David Jones,
153 New Street,
Ealing
London
3
It's in a suburb called Ealing. Would you like a taxi?
LIFT
MARY
Yes, please.
4
What number is it?
A hundred and fifty-three.
5
Hello. Nice to see you. Come in, please.
153
Hello, David.
6
This is my wife, Susan.
How do you do?
7
And these are our children – Mary and Charles.
Hello.
8
Would you like some more tea?
No. Thank you. I've had enough.
9
Have another sandwich.
No thanks. I'm full.
10
It's a nice garden. It's very green.
Yes, I like gardening.
11
The weather is quite good. Let's sit here.
Yes. Have a seat.
12
What funny weather you have here!

UNIT

3 My Life

Lesson 1 I live in Doha

1 Listen and read

My name's Jameel Salah. I'm Qatari. I was born in Doha in 1975. I live on the Corniche Road. My apartment is near the sea. I live with my wife, my two sons and my wife's mother. I'm an accountant and I work for a small company in Doha. The name of the company is ARK Limited. In the evenings I study English at the Gulf Language School. I like learning English, but I don't have a lot of free time.

I'm Khadija Saeed. I'm from Cairo and I'm Egyptian. I was born in 1985. I was born in a suburb of Cairo called Heliopolis, but I don't live there now. I live in Zamalek with my parents and my three sisters. We have a small flat near the River Nile. I'm a secretary and I work for a company called Egypt Tours. In my free time I like playing tennis and learning about Egyptian history.

2 Write

Name: *Jameel Salah*
Born: ______ Year: ______
Live: ______
Job: ______
Company: ______

Name: ______
Born: ______ Year: ______
Live: ______
Job: ______
Company: ______

3 Listen and say

Where do you live?
Do you live in London?

4 Ask and answer

Ask five people.

A	B
Where do you live?	I live in ...

	NAME	DISTRICT/CITY
1	______	______
2	______	______
3	______	______
4	______	______
5	______	______

LOOK!

do and don't

I	live ...	
You	work ...	
We	have ...	
	like ...	
I	don't	live ...
You		work ...
We		have ...
		like...
Do	I	live ... ?
	you	work ...?
	we	have ...?
		like ...?

Where do you live? I live in ...

LOOK!

The verbs: *have* and *have got*

I **have** two children/I **have got** two children.

I **don't have**/I **haven't got** much time.

Do you have/**Have you got** a car?

5 Match

Match the sentences with the pictures.

a I live in a small house.
b I work in an office.
c I don't have much time.
d I like playing tennis.

6 Write

Write in these words: **in**, **live**, **do**, **flat**, **have**, **don't**

A: Where (a) __________ you live, Khadija?

K: In Cairo.

A: Do you (b) __________ in the centre?

K: Yes. I live (c) __________ Zamalek.

A: Do you (d) __________ a house?

K: No, we (e) __________. We have a small (f) __________.

Write in these words: **don't**, **have**, **am**, **do**, **like**, **are**

B: (g) __________ you from Saudi Arabia, Jameel?

J: No, I'm not. I (h) __________ from Qatar.

B: (i) __________ you live in Doha?

J: Yes, I do. We (j) __________ an apartment near the sea.

B: Do you (k) __________ living in an apartment?

J: No, I (l) __________. It's very small.

LANGUAGE

Present Simple Tense: I, you, we
Verbs: to live, to work, to study, to have
have/have got
a lot of

Lesson 2 Where do you work?

1 Listen and write

Write **A**, **B**, **C** or **D**.

ARRIVALS

A
Which country are you from?
We're from Thailand.
And where do you work?
Here in Muscat. We work for LBC Motors. We're mechanics.

B
What's your job, Tony?
I'm a teacher.
Which subject do you teach?
English. I work for the Capital English School.

C
Do you work in Riyadh, Susan?
No, I don't, I work in Dhahran in a hospital.
Which hospital?
The Awal Hospital.
And what do you do?
I'm a doctor.

D
Where do you work, Adel?
Here. At the Airport.
Are you a steward?
No. I work in an office. I'm an accountant.

2 What are their jobs?

a Tony is ________ ________ .
b The two men from Thailand are ________.
c The woman is ________ ________.
d Adel is ________ ________.

LOOK!

Where do you work?

In	an office. a factory. Dubai.
For	ABC Limited. an engineering company. my uncle.
At	the airport.

3 Match

Match the job with the company/place.

a bus driver
b steward (stewardess)
c mechanic
d teacher
e businessman (woman)
f cashier

Middle East Airlines

ATIF'S MOTORS

HABIB BANK

AWAL TRADING COMPANY

MANAMA GIRLS' SECONDARY SCHOOL

Express Transport Company

4 Ask and answer

Choose a job from the list above. Now ask and answer.

A: Where do you work?

B: I work at...
I work for ...
I work in ...

A: What do you do?
What's your job?

B: I'm a ...

LOOK!

Which?
A: Where do you work?
B: In a hospital.
A: **Which** hospital?
B: The Awal Hospital.
Which subject do you teach?
Which company do you work for?

5 Listen and say

Sounds and spelling. Listen.
b**u**siness, b**u**sinessman — a woman, two w**o**men
Say these words. They all have the "**i**" sound.
b**u**siness, w**o**men, wh**i**ch, w**i**th, s**i**t, **i**n, **E**nglish

AWAL HOSPITAL
ENTRANCE

6 Listen and say

Say the '**er**' sound. The '**r**' is silent!
work, **word**, **her**, **third**, **nurse**, **learn**, **first**, **shirt**, **earth**, **German**, **Germany**

A: I'm a nurse.
B: A nurse? Where do you work?
A: I work in Germany.
B: In Germany? Are you German?
A: Yes, I'm a German nurse!

LANGUAGE

I work for ...	Which company ...?
I work in ...	Which country ...?
I work at ...	Verbs: to do, to teach
Which ...?	What do you do?

Lesson 3 My children go to school

1 Read

Helen is with Lara's cousin, Sally. It is Thursday morning and they are in the park with Sally's children.

Helen: How old are your children, Sally?
Sally: Well, Ben is seven and Joe is eight – and little Nina is eighteen months.
Helen: Which one is Ben?
Sally: That's Ben – there. The one with brown hair.
Helen: Oh I see – on the swing. Do the boys go to school?
Sally: Yes, they do.
Helen: Do they like it?
Sally: Yes, they do. They love it. They're very happy there.
Helen: Really? Which school do they go to?
Sally: Park Lane Primary School.
Helen: What's it like? Is it new?
Sally: Yes, it's new and it's quite big. I think it's very good.

Put a tick or a cross.

a Sally has two children. ☐
b Ben is on the swing. ☐
c Ben and Joe go to a primary school. ☐
d They don't like school very much. ☐
e The school is a new school. ☐

LOOK!
primary school
intermediate school
secondary school

SCHOOL

2 Match

Match these verbs with the pictures: **love**, **hate**, **like**, **don't like**

______ ______ ______ ______

3 Look and say

I love, like, don't like, hate

For example: I don't like ice-cream.
I hate driving.

4 Write

Write in these words: **hate**, **go**, **they**, **don't**

A: Do your children (a) ______ to school?
B: Yes, (b) ______ do, but they (c) ______ like it.
A: No? Why not?
B: Because they are lazy! They (d) ______ studying.

Write in these words: **but**, **to**, **Secondary**, **subjects**, **love**, **which**

C: (e) ______ school do you go (f) ______, girls?
D: Newton Girls' (g) ______ School.
C: And which (h) ______ do you like?
E: I like mathematics and Arabic, (i) ______ I don't like science. It's boring.
C: And you, Lulwa?
D: I like geography and I (j) ______ history. I think it's great!

5 Listen and say

These words all have the 'A' sound:

gate, **late**, **hate**, **wait**, **lazy**, **play**, **eight**, **grey**, **say**, **name**, **baby**, **date**, **radio**, **snake**

Now say these words with the 'e' sound:

get, **let**, **secondary**, **centre**, **secretary**, **subject**, **tennis**, **relative**, **cigarette**

LANGUAGE

Present Simple Tense: they
which one?
Verbs: to go, to hate, to love

Lesson 4 Peter's school

1 Listen and read

1
My name's Peter Parker. I teach English at the Capital English School.
2
This is my classroom. Come in and have a seat.
3
Show me your homework please, Mike.
I'm sorry. It's at home.
4
Open your books.
Which page?
5
I haven't got a book.
Let John look at your book, Dan.
6
Close that window please, Tom. It's noisy outside.
7
Be quiet, please Mike! Listen to this.

2 Match

Match the verbs with the pictures: **show**, **give**, **open**, **close**

a

____

b

____

c

____

d

____

LOOK!

Open	the book.	
Close	the window.	
Show	me	your homework.
Give	him	the book.
	her	
	Mike	

3 Match

Match these words with the pictures: **pen**, **keys**, **book**, **money**, **paper**, **photograph**

4 Look and say

Ask your partners.

Give	me	the watch.
Show	him	money.
	her	etc
	Mohsin	
	Nora	

20 EURO
10 EURO
5 EURO

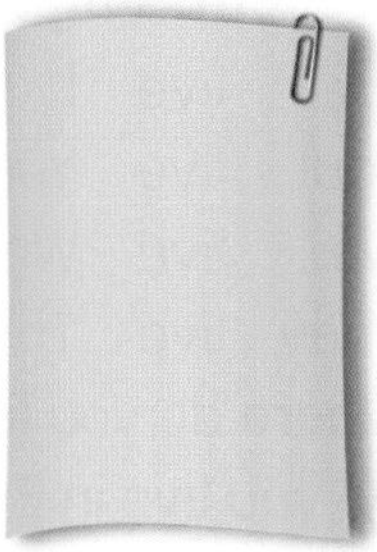

5 Write

Write: **me**, **her** or **him**

a That's my pen! Give it to ________.

b Khalid's hungry. Give ________ some sandwiches.

c There's a guard at the gate. Show ________ your permit.

d Mrs Brown isn't very well. Give ________ some water.

e Who are you? Show ________ your identification card.

f I think that's Lulwa's handbag. Give it to ________.

LOOK!

Give Nora the pen.
Give **her** the pen.
Give the pen to **her**.

6 Listen and say

Sounds and spelling
photograph, **f**ull, enou**gh**

7 Listen

Tick the sentence you hear.

a Where's my cap? ☐
Where's my cab? ☐

b What a beautiful peach! ☐
What a beautiful beach! ☐

c Be careful! There's a pea on your chair. ☐
Be careful! There's a bee on your chair. ☐

d Where's my pen? ☐
Where's my Ben? ☐

LANGUAGE

Object pronouns: me, him, her
Verbs: to give, to open, to close

Give	me
Show	him
	her

Be quiet!

STUDY

Present Simple Tense – verb: *to live*

I	live	I	don't live	Do I live ...?
You	live	You	don't live	Do you live ...?
We	live	We	don't live	Do we live ...?
They	live	They	don't live	Do they live ...?

Where do you live?
Do you live in Beirut? Yes, I do.
No, I don't.

Which?

Which car would you like?
Which school do you go to?
Which country are you from?
Which one is Ben?

Object pronouns: *me, you, him, her*

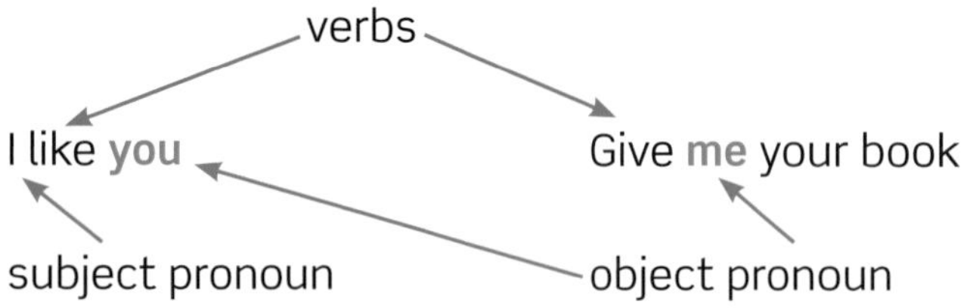
verbs
I like you
Give me your book
subject pronoun
object pronoun

Subject	Object
I	me
you	you
he	him
she	her

a lot of

I don't have much time.
I don't have many friends.
I don't have **a lot of** time.
I don't have **a lot of** friends.

NEW WORDS

Learn these words.

Verbs
to live
to work
to play
to learn
to go
to love
to hate
to open
to close
to give

Adjectives
quiet
noisy
boring
lazy

Jobs
accountant
businessman
cashier
steward
stewardess

Subjects
history
mathematics
geography
science
Arabic

Schools
primary
intermediate
secondary

Other
factory
watch
photograph
paper
company
apartment
tennis
page
sea
flat
window
homework
Middle East
trading
transport
motor

Animals
elephant
monkey
fish
camel
snake

Write other new words here.

______________________________ ______________________________

______________________________ ______________________________

______________________________ ______________________________

______________________________ ______________________________

______________________________ ______________________________

______________________________ ______________________________

______________________________ ______________________________

4 Family And Friends

Lesson 1 My brother lives in Beirut

1 **Listen and read**

This is my brother, Ali. He was born in Kuwait, but he lives in Beirut. He's a student at the American University of Beirut. He studies Medicine.

And this is a photo of my grandfather, Eyad. He's very clever. He speaks four languages – Arabic, English, Farsi and Urdu. He also speaks a little French.

This is my younger sister Eman. I like her very much. She's very sweet and kind. She's only sixteen, so she's still at school. She goes to secondary school.

And this is my older brother, Abdul Karim. He's very nice, too. He's a security guard and he works in a bank. He likes fishing in his free time. Sometimes he catches a fish!

2 **Match**

Write the names.

a Who likes fishing? ____________________

b Who studies medicine? ____________________

c Who speaks four languages? ____________________

d Who still goes to school? ____________________

LOOK!

I	live	They	live
You	live	He	lives
We	live	She	lives

LOOK!

s

live	+	s	=	lives
work	+	s	=	works
study	+	ies	=	studies
go	+	es	=	goes
teach	+	es	=	teaches

3 Write

Write in these verbs: **likes**, **speaks**, **goes**, **lives**, **studies**, **works**

a Steve __________ in a house near the market.

b My cousin __________ for a big bank.

c Nadia __________ playing the piano.

d My friend __________ English very well.

e Hassan __________ History at Cairo University.

f My daughter, Jenny, __________ to primary school.

4 Listen and say

These verbs end in the '**sss**' sound: **likes**, **works**, **hates**, **speaks**
These verbs end in the '**zzz**' sound: **lives**, **loves**, **studies**, **plays**, **goes**, **has**
These verbs end in the '**iz**' sound: **teaches**, **watches**, **catches**

5 Look and say

Use the verbs: **lives**, **works** (**for**/**in**)

Example: Sam lives in Dallas. He works for an American oil company.

Sam (Dallas – an oil company)

Tom (Amman – the Habib Bank)

Hassan (Aswan – a hotel)

Gary (Madrid – a shopping centre)

Mary (Rome – an office)

Sarah (Athens – a hospital)

Leila (Sur – a secondary school)

John (London – ABC Limited)

Peter (Bahrain – Capital English School)

Mohammad (Dammam – a ministry)

Lesson 2 A Wedding Party

1 Listen and read

Lina is at a friend's wedding party. Sarah is her guest.

Lina: Would you like some more juice, Sarah?

Sarah: Yes, please. Who's that woman, Lina?

Lina: Which one?

Sarah: The one in the red dress.

Lina: Oh, that's Kamila. She's my cousin.

Sarah: Does she live here in Sur?

Lina: No. She doesn't live in Oman. She lives in Saudi Arabia. In Jeddah.

Sarah: Why's that?

Lina: Well, her husband is from Jeddah.

Sarah: I see. She's very pretty.

Lina: Yes, she is. She's clever too. She's a lecturer.

Sarah: Where does she work?

Lina: At King Abdul Aziz University in Jeddah.

Sarah: And which subject does she teach?

Lina: I'm not sure. Come on. Let's ask her!

Put a tick (✓), a cross (✗) or D (for 'don't know').

a Kamila is Lina's cousin. ☐

b Kamila lives in Sur in Oman. ☐

c Kamila's husband is from Saudi Arabia. ☐

d Kamila is a university lecturer. ☐

e She teaches mathematics. ☐

LOOK!

does

Kamila lives in Jeddah.
Does she live in Oman?
She **doesn't** live in Oman.
(She **does** not live in Oman.)

do/does

I			I	live ...?
You			you	
We	don't live ...	Do	we	
They			they	
She/He	doesn't live	Does	she/he	live ...?

2 Write

These sentences are not true. Write them out with **doesn't**.

Example: Sarah likes cooking. Sarah doesn't like cooking.

a Kamila lives in Muscat. ______________________

b Kamila works in a hospital. ______________________

c Lina teaches in a university. ______________________

d Sarah speaks Arabic very well. ______________________

e Lina knows her cousin very well. ______________________

3 Read

Read more about Kamila.

Kamila is married to Jaber and they live in Jeddah in Saudi Arabia. She is a lecturer at the university and she teaches science. They have three children, two girls and a boy. She speaks three languages – Arabic, English and French. She also speaks a little Turkish.

4 Ask and answer

Ask questions with **does** about Kamila.

	A			B
Does	Kamila	live	...?	Yes, she does.
		work		No, she doesn't.
		teach		
		speak		
		have		

Example: Does Kamila live in Oman? No, she doesn't.

Now ask questions with **is**.

A		B
Is she	married?	Yes, she is.
	a doctor?	No, she isn't.
	clever?	
	from Saudi Arabia?	
	Lina's sister?	

5 Match

Match these words with the pictures of the clothes:

a red dress	a blue jacket	a brown skirt	gold shoes	a green and yellow shirt
grey trousers	a red cap	a white T-shirt	a black suit	

LANGUAGE

Present Simple Tense: does/doesn't
the one...
also/too/both
Vocabulary: clothes, colours

Lesson 3 Shopping

1 Listen and write

Write A, B, C or D.

A
How much is that jacket, please?
Sixty dollars.
Sixty or sixteen?
Sixty.
Oh that's too much.

B
I'd like that dress.
The blue and yellow one?
No. The green and pink one. Is it expensive?
No. It only costs forty pounds.
I'll take it please.

C
How much is that car?
Which one?
The blue and silver sports car.
Ah yes. It's a beautiful car and it's not very old.
Yes, but how much does it cost?
Five thousand five hundred dollars. It's a bargain!

D
I'd like some white shirts.
How many?
Three I think. How much are they?
Ten riyals each.
OK. I'll have three please.

2 Write

a The jacket costs ________.

b The dress costs ________.

c The shirts cost ________ each.

d The sports car costs ________.

3 Listen and say

How much is that car?
How much does it cost?

LOOK!

it
How much does **it** cost?
It costs ...

4 Listen and say

Numbers: 1,000 - 10,000

1,000 – **a thousand**, 2,000 – **two thousand**, 2,500 – **two thousand five hundred**, 5,300 – **five thousand three hundred**, 9,800 – **nine thousand eight hundred**

5 Ask and answer

A

How much is the ...?
How much does the ... cost?

B

... riyals
dinars
dirhams
pounds
dollars

LOOK!

3,450 = three thousand four hundred and fifty

Price list A
dress – 1,500 riyals
car
cap – 240 dirhams
camera – 3,300 riyals
shirt
picture
watch – 8,900 dirhams
jacket

Price list B
dress
car – 6,700 dinars
cap
camera
shirt – 480 dirhams
picture – 1,200 riyals
watch
jacket – 2,500 pounds

MV56 UVJ

6 Act it out!

A You want to buy a camera. You have only 5,000 dirhams.

B You have a camera. The price is 6,000 dirhams.

A You have a car. The price is 2,500 dinars.

B You want to buy a car. You only have 2,200 dinars.

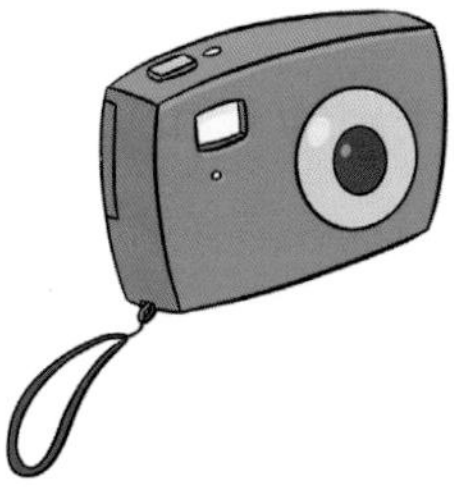

Use these words:

How much is...? How much does ... cost?

That's too much! It's a bargain. That's cheap/expensive.

It's very good/old ... my last price!

7 Listen and say

These words have the letter 'r'

price, **trousers**, **grey**, **dress**, **green**, **primary**, **street**, **brother**

The 'r' is silent in these words:

sports car, **far**, **party**, **arm**, **Mars**, **car park**, **bargain**

LANGUAGE

Present Simple Tense: it
It costs ...
How much does it cost?
Numbers: 1,000 – 10,000
Verb: to cost

Lesson 4 Congratulations!

1 Read and match

a Congratulations!
b This is my brother-in-law, Harry. He comes from Cardiff.
c Harry has a new baby daughter.
d Pleased to meet you. How do you do?

2 Listen and say

congratulations

brother-in-law

LOOK!

brother-in-law	mother-in-law	son-in-law
sister-in-law	father-in-law	daughter-in-law

3 Look and say

A	B
I've got a new job!	Well done!
I've got my driving licence.	That's excellent!
	great!
	very good!
	fantastic!
	Congratulations!
It's my birthday today.	Happy Birthday!

4 Match

Match the relatives:

cousin, **grandfather**, **son-in-law**, **grandson**, **daughter-in-law**, **uncle**, **brother-in-law**, **sister**

a your son's wife
b your father's brother
c your daughter's son
d your husband's brother
e your mother's father
f your aunt's daughter
g your daughter's husband
h your brother's sister

LOOK!

Verb: *to come from*

Where are you from?	I'm from Saudi Arabia.
Where **do** you **come** from?	I **come** from Saudi Arabia.

5 Write

Write in these words: **do**, **well done**, **meet**, **come**, **got**, **sister-in-law**

A: This is my (a) __________, Salwa.

B: How (b) __________ you do?

C: Pleased to (c) __________ you.

B: Where do you (d) __________ from, Salwa?

C: From Syria.

A: Salwa (e) __________ a new job today.

B: Really? (f) __________!

Write in these words: **wife**, **congratulations**, **have**, **boy**, **birthday**

A: (g) __________ a piece of cake, Sam.

B: Thanks. Is it your (h) __________?

A: No. My (i) __________ and I have a new baby.

B: (j) __________! A boy or a girl?

A: A (k) __________. His name's Alex.

6 Listen and say

Say these long words. Where is the 'stress'? Put a (✗).

congratulations, university, primary school, intermediate, secondary

engineering, mathematics, Happy Birthday, Middle East Airlines

LANGUAGE

congratulations, well done, excellent, great, fantastic, Happy Birthday
Relatives: ... -in-law
Verb: to come from

STUDY

Present Simple Tense – verb: *to live*

He	lives	He	doesn't live	Does he	live ...?
She	lives	She	doesn't live	Does she	live ...?
It	lives	It	doesn't live	Does it	live ...?

Where does he live?
Does he live in Beirut? Yes, he does.
No, he doesn't.

was/were

I	was	born
You	were	born
He	was	born
She	was	born

Where was he born?
Where was she born?

good/well

He's a **good** football player.
He plays football **well**.

too/also/both

Ann Barry likes cooking and writing letters.

She likes learning English **too**.
She **also** likes learning English.

Hassan and his brother **both** work in a restaurant.
They are **both** waiters.

The one ...

Who's that funny man?
Which man?
The one in the red and white cap.

Who's that woman?
Which woman?
The one in the red dress.

NEW WORDS

Learn these words.

Colours
pink
silver
gold

Adjectives
clever
kind
nice
funny
younger
older
pretty

Clothes
trousers
shirt
skirt
suit
shoes
dress

Other
great
fantastic
excellent
well done
congratulations
sweet
It's a bargain.
It's too much.
Last price!

Verbs
to teach
to watch
to catch
to cost
to come from

Relatives
brother-in-law
sister-in-law
father-in-law
mother-in-law
son-in-law
daughter-in-law

Animals
horse
dog
cat

Jobs
trader
security guard
lecturer
singer

Other
wedding
party
price
sports car

Write other new words here.

Revision B

Grammar

The Present Simple Tense: *to be*

I	am	I	am not	Am I ...?
You	are	You	are not	Are you ...?
He	is	He	is not	Is he ...?
She	is	She	is not	Is she ...?
It	is	It	is not	Is it ...?
We	are	We	are not	Are we ...?
They	are	They	are not	Are they ...?

1 Write

Write: **am (‘m)**, **are (‘re)**, **is (‘s)**, **am not (‘m not)**, **are not (aren’t)** or **is not (isn’t)** in the spaces.

a ‘Where ________ you from?’ ‘I ________ from Baghdad.’

b ‘________ Tim and Alex relatives?’ ‘No, they ________. They ________ friends.’

c ‘________ Sudan quite small?’ ‘No, it ________. It ________ very big.’

d ‘________ you a visitor?’ ‘No, I ________. I work here.’

e ‘________ your sister a doctor?’ ‘Yes, she ________.’

f ‘What ________ the school like?’ ‘It ________ new.’

g ‘You ________ late!’ ‘Yes. I ________ sorry.’

h ‘________ you hungry?’ ‘No, we ________.’

The Present Simple Tense: *to live*

I	live	I	don’t live	Do	I	live ...?
You		You			you	
We		We			we	
They		They			they	
He	lives	He	doesn’t live	Does	he	live ...?
She		She			she	
It		It			it	

2 Write

Put the verbs in the Present Simple form.

My name (a) ________ (be) Ali Abdulla. I (b) ________ (live) in a village in Bahrain. It (c) ________ (be) about 25 kilometres from Manama. I (d) ________ (be) a farmer, but I (e) ________ (not work) very much now. I (f) ________ (be) quite old! I (g) ________ (have) five children and three grandchildren. My son, Omar, (h) ________ (be) a clerk. He (i) ________ (work) in the Ministry of Education. My other son, Rashid, (j) ________ (not work). He (k) ________ (go) to Hamad Town Secondary School. Omar (l) ________ (live) with my brother in Manama. My daughter, Fatin, (m) ________ (study) Arabic at the university. She still (n) ________ (live) here with me in the village. My other daughters (o) ________ (be) married. They (p) ________ (live) in another village not far from here. Najwa (q) ________ (have) three beautiful children.

3 Write

Write **don't** or **doesn't** in these sentences.

a I'm sorry. I ________ speak English very well.

b My brother ________ catch many fish.

c We ________ live in Heliopolis now. We live in Zamalek.

d John ________ work in the kitchen. He's a waiter.

e This sports car ________ cost very much. It's a bargain!

f My children ________ go to school. They are too young.

g Simon Star is very busy. He ________ have time for hobbies.

h No. I ________ teach Arabic. I study Arabic.

i Fatima ________ like her new office very much. It's too small.

j Dan's brother-in-law ________ come from London. He comes from Cardiff.

k Tom and Mary ________ watch television in the evening. They read.

l My sister and I ________ study history. We study mathematics and science.

4 Write

Simon Star is in a television studio in Cairo. Write **do** or **does** in this dialogue.

Aida: Welcome to Cairo, Mr Star.

Simon: Thank you. Call me Simon, please.

Aida: All right, Simon. (a) ________ you like our city?

Simon: (b) ________ I like it? I love it. I think it's great.

Aida: I know you are from America, but which city (c) ________ you come from?

Simon: I was born in New York, but I live in Los Angeles now.

Aida: And where (d) ________ your wife come from?

Simon: She's from Miami.

Aida: What (e) ________ she do?

Simon: She's an actress. She's with me in Cairo now.

Aida: (f) ________ she like visiting different countries?

Simon: She loves it. She likes going to markets.

Aida: How many children (g) ________ you have?

Simon: We have two – John and Betty. They're here in Cairo too.

Aida: (h) ________ your children like watching basketball?

Simon: John likes basketball, but Betty thinks it's boring.

Aida: (i) ________ they go to basketball games?

Simon: Sometimes, yes.

Aida: Finally, Mr St ... I mean, Simon. What (j) ________ you do in your free time?

Simon: What (k) ________ I do? Nothing. Just swimming and resting.

5 Write

Put in the pronouns: **I, you, he, she, me, you, him, or her**

Pronouns

Subject	**Object**
I	me
you	you
he	him
she	her

________ like ________.
Do ________ like ________?

Show ________ our passports, Mary.
________ is the immigration officer.
IMMIGRATION

Give ________ your seat.
________ is tired.

New Words

6 Verbs

Match the verbs with the pictures:
live, **open**, **work**, **study**, **play**, **go**, **love**, **hate**, **teach**, **watch**, **close**, **cost**

a ________

b ________

c ________

d ________

e ________

$25
f ________

g ________

h ________

i ________

j ________

k ________

l ________

7 Animals

Find and circle nine animals in the square. Write the words.

R	P	M	V	I	K	F	C
C	H	O	R	S	E	I	A
A	G	N	E	B	S	S	T
M	Z	K	O	E	N	H	X
E	L	E	P	H	A	N	T
L	B	Y	G	U	K	I	J
A	D	T	I	G	E	R	M
C	F	U	D	O	G	Z	C

1 ________
2 ________
3 ________
4 ________
5 ________
6 ________
7 ________
8 ________
9 ________

8 Clothes

Match the words with the pictures: **trousers**, **shirt**, **skirt**, **suit**, **shoes**, **dress**, **hat**, **cap**, **overalls**, **uniform**

a	________	f	________
b	________	g	________
c	________	h	________
d	________	i	________
e	________	j	________

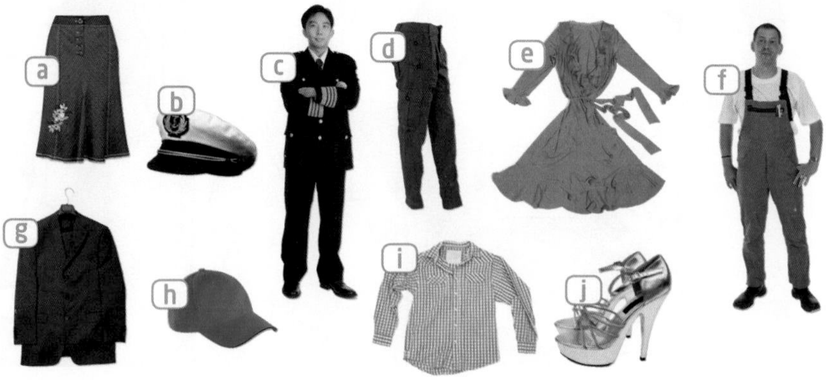
a
b
c
d
e
f
g
h
i
j

9 Write

Write these words in the sentences:

price, **apartment**, **company**, **secondary**, **wedding**, **photograph**, **watch**, **steward**

a 'What's the time?' 'Sorry. I haven't got a ________.'

b This is a ________ of my baby daughter, Amina.

c Ali is a businessman. He works for his uncle's ________.

d Hamid has got a job with Gulf Air. He's a ________.

e Give me 1,000 pounds for the car. That's my last ________!

f There is a big ________ party at the Good Luck Hotel.

g We live in a small ________ near the city centre.

h Badria teaches in a ________ school in Kuwait.

Punctuation

10 Write out the paragraph with the correct punctuation.

my names pierre and im twenty-three years old im from paris and im a student at paris university i study science and mathematics i study english too but i don't speak it very well my wifes name is laura she doesn't come from france shes greek shes also a student and she studies art and history we don't have any children we live with my parents in a district of paris called pigalle in my free time i like playing basketball

____

____

____

____

____

____

____

____

Spelling

11 Look

There are two spelling mistakes in every line.

a lives, teaches, studyes, loves, costes, works, has, plays
b who, where, whach, why, whate, whose, how
c kind, sweet, noisy, lasy, boring, claver, pretty
d give, sit, opin, close, have, come, showe
e Middel East Airlines, Awal Trading Company, Expres Transport

There are five mistakes in this dialogue.

A: This is a great partey.
B: Yes, it is. Who's that funny man over thare?
A: Which one?
B: The very fat one in the pink and white shert.
A: That's my brother-in-low!
B: I'm very sarry!

Pronunciation

12 Match the words that have the same sounds

Match the words that have the same sounds.

teach, work, gate, get, car, both, shoe, dog

shirt, free, eight, dress, party, too, open, watch

Read and Write

13 Read

Read about these people. Match the names and nationalities.

Akbar	French
Marie	Japanese
Mustapha	Indian
Yoshioa	Egyptian

A

Akbar is a taxi driver. He lives in Mumbai in India, but he was born in Delhi in the north. His son is a mechanic and he works in Qatar. Akbar meets many tourists. He drives them from the airport to their hotels. He doesn't speak Arabic, but he knows a few words of English. In his free time he likes reading poetry.

B

Marie Dupont is an actress. She is famous for her films about the history of France. She doesn't like big cities and lives in a quiet village near Paris. She travels a lot because she makes films all over the world. At the moment she is in Lebanon.

C

Mustapha Habib is a footballer. He is Egyptian, but he lives in Munich in Germany. He plays football for a club in Germany. He is a striker and scores many goals. He has a house in Munich, but he doesn't live there in the summer. He goes to Cairo in May, at the end of the football season. He is married and has three children.

D

Yoshioa Masaoka is a businessman. He works for a Japanese car company. He travels to the Middle East many times every year. His company sells a lot of cars to Arab countries. Yoshioa lives in Tokyo in Japan. He likes learning languages. He speaks English and German quite well, but he doesn't speak much Arabic.

Write the correct names in the sentences: *Akbar, Marie, Mustapha, Yoshioa.*

a ____________ was born in Delhi.

b ____________ plays football in Germany.

c ____________ doesn't like big cities.

d ____________ lives in Cairo in the summer.

e ____________ is in Lebanon at the moment.

f ____________ likes reading poetry in his free time.

g ____________ works for a car company.

h ____________ and ____________ don't speak much Arabic.

14 Write about these people.

Name:	Samia Saeedi	Khalid Mohammad
Born:	Alexandria	Al Ain
Year:	1981	1989
Married/Single:	married – one daughter	single
Lives:	Cairo, Egypt	Dubai
Job:	accountant	cashier
Company:	Al Ahlia Trading	Gulf Bank
Free time/hobbies:	learning French, writing to friends	playing table-tennis, swimming, computers

Story: Hello London 5

David and his friends are visiting London Zoo.

1
Welcome to the ZOO
How much is it?
Twenty pounds each, please.
2
ELEPHANTS
DO NOT FEED THE ANIMALS
3
SNAKES
MONKEYS
TIGERS
CAMELS
Let's see the tigers now.
Yes, please.
4
Help! Help! My son!
5
Ali! What're you doing?
6
Thank you very much. You were so brave.
It was nothing.
7
Where do you come from?
I'm from Dubai. I'm here on holiday with my grandfather. It's our first visit to London.
8
And what do you do in Dubai?
I'm a student. I study Engineering at a college in Dubai.
9
Tell me about your grandfather. Does he come from Dubai too?
Yes he does, but he was born in Al Ain. He's a businessman and he has a small company in Dubai.
10
Let's go! I don't like all these questions!
EXIT
11
Look at this, Ali. You're famous!
12
EVENING NEW
TOURIST HERO SAVES BOY FROM TIGER

5 When?

Lesson 1 My Day

I work here – in the refinery. The work is quite hard and the hours are long, but the money's good. I start work early, at seven o'clock in the morning, so I usually have breakfast in the canteen. I finish work at about six in the evening and then I have dinner with my family. I sometimes work on the night shift, but I don't like that very much.

1 Listen and read

a Where does Alan work?
b When does he start work?
c When does he finish?
d Does he usually have breakfast at home?
e Does he sometimes work at night?

LOOK!

Times

half past four or four thirty

2 Match

Match these times with the clocks and watches:

six thirty, **eleven o'clock**, **half past three**, **five o'clock**, **half past twelve**, **seven o'clock**, **one thirty**, **half past nine**.

1:30

3 Look and say

I start	work school college university	at ...
I finish at ...		

4 Listen and say

When do you have breakfast?
When do you have lunch?
When do you have dinner?

LOOK!

I have breakfast ...
lunch
dinner

5 Ask and answer

Ask three people.

A: When do you have breakfast?
B: At eight o'clock.

When do you have lunch?
At half past one.

When do you have dinner?
At six thirty.

LOOK!

sometimes/usually

I (don't)	usually	have breakfast in the canteen.
I	sometimes	work on the night shift.

Name	Times		
	breakfast	lunch	dinner
1 ______	______	______	______
2 ______	______	______	______
3 ______	______	______	______

6 Write

Write out these sentences with **sometimes** or **usually**.

a Samia has breakfast with her children. (sometimes)

______

b Tom and Mary go to England in the summer. (usually)

______

c I don't watch television in the evening. (usually)

______

d My brother-in-law plays football for the A club. (sometimes)

______

e We have dinner at eight o'clock. (usually)

______

f My cousin and I go shopping in the afternoon. (sometimes)

______

7 Listen and say

Say the '**st**' sound.

start, **st**op, **st**airs, **st**udent, **st**udy, **st**ation, **st**ereo, **st**reet

LANGUAGE

When ...?
sometimes/usually
Times: half past six, six thirty
Verbs: to start, to finish, to have

Lesson 2 What do you have for breakfast?

1 Match

Match these words with the pictures: **cheese**, **jam**, **eggs**, **olives**, **yoghurt**

a 
b 
c 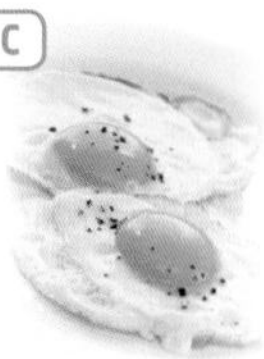
d 
e 

2 Listen

Listen and write A, B, C or D.

A
When do you usually get up, Simon?
Late! About eight thirty or a quarter to nine.
And what do you have for breakfast?
Coffee, eggs and orange juice.

B
Do you usually get up early, Liz?
Yes, quite early. I get up about quarter past seven.
Do you? And what about breakfast?
I never have breakfast. Just tea.

C
What's the food like in the canteen, Alan?
It's not bad. I have my breakfast there.
What do you have?
Tea, bread and jam, or sometimes cheese and olives.

Canteen

D
What time do you get up in the morning, Mary?
Quite early, about six fifteen. I never get up late.
And what about breakfast?
Just fruit and yoghurt usually.

What do they have for breakfast? Put a tick (✓)

	tea	coffee	bread	fruit	jam	yoghurt	eggs	orange juice	cheese	olives
Simon	☐	☐	☐	☐	☐	☐	☐	☐	☐	☐
Liz	☐	☐	☐	☐	☐	☐	☐	☐	☐	☐
Alan	☐	☐	☐	☐	☐	☐	☐	☐	☐	☐
Mary	☐	☐	☐	☐	☐	☐	☐	☐	☐	☐

LOOK!

When ...?/What time ...?

When do you get up in the morning?
What time do you get up in the morning?

LOOK!

Time

a quarter past eleven
eleven fifteen

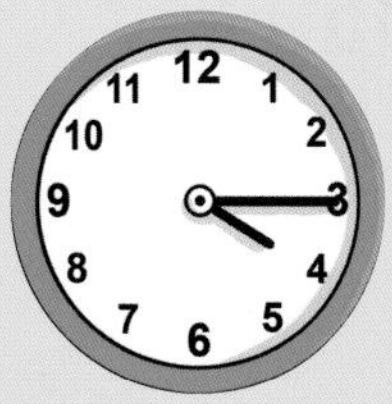

a quarter past four
four fifteen

3 Look and say

What's the time? It's ...

a
b
c
d
e
f
g
h
i
j
k
l

4 Write

Write in the words: **usually**, **sometimes** or **never**

a Liz ________________ has breakfast. Just tea.

b Alan ________________ has breakfast in the canteen.

c He ________________ has cheese and olives for breakfast.

d Mary ________________ gets up late.

e Alan ________________ works at night.

f Liz ________________ gets up at about a quarter past seven.

5 Look and say

Talk about your morning.

I	usually sometimes never	get up ... have ... for breakfast. start work/school ...

Lesson 3 Tom's day

1 Read

Number the pictures.

Tom always gets up early and goes for a run. After that he has a shower and gets dressed. Then he has a big breakfast – eggs, toast, tea and fruit juice. At about half past seven he leaves home and drives to the bank. He usually finishes work about two thirty and then he returns home. He has lunch with his wife, Mary. In the afternoon he always rests for an hour and then he goes for a walk before dinner. In the evening Tom and Mary stay at home. Tom usually reads and then he goes to bed at about ten.

11:22
6:00
BANK

2 Match

Match the verbs with the pictures above.
get up, stay (at home), walk, go (to bed), finish (work), have (breakfast), run, start (work)

LOOK!

to leave (home)

to return (home)

3 Write

Write the verbs in the text in the "**s**" form.

Liz (a) __________ at seven fifteen. She (b) __________ just cup of tea for breakfast. She (c) __________ home about a quarter to eight and (d) __________ to work. At eleven o'clock she usually (e) __________ tea and a sandwich. She (f) __________ work at three o'clock and then (g) __________ home. In the evening she usually (h) __________ at home with her family, but sometimes she (i) __________ friends or relatives.

4 Write

Write sentences with **always**, **usually**, **sometimes** or **never**

Example: coffee / for breakfast
I never have coffee for breakfast.

a get up / late ____________

b rice / for lunch ____________

c stay at home / evening ____________

d friends / afternoon ____________

e tea / at night ____________

f go shopping / morning ____________

g go to bed / early ____________

LOOK!

always

I	always usually sometimes	get up have
He She	never	gets up has

5 Look and say

Tell the story of Sarah's day.

SUPERMARKET

6 Listen and write

Write the verbs in the correct lists: **returns**, **walks**, **leaves**, **rests**, **visits**, **stays**, **reads**, **gets**, **drives**

'ssss': likes, ____

'zzzz': lives, ____

LANGUAGE

always

then / and then	to go to (bed)
after / before	to go for (a run)
Verbs: to get dressed, to rest, to return, to leave, to run, to read, to walk, to drive, to stay	to go for (a walk) to have (a shower)

Lesson 4 Peter's week

1 Listen

SPORT

Peter is on a plane. He's going on holiday.

Farouq: Where do you work?
Peter: In Bahrain. I'm a teacher in a language school.
Farouq: Really? I'm a teacher too. How many classes do you have?
Peter: Four classes every day – two in the morning and two in the evening.
Farouq: So you don't teach in the afternoons?
Peter: No. But every Monday and Wednesday afternoon I go to my Arabic lessons.
Farouq: Oh, you teach Arabic too?
Peter: Oh no! I study it. I'm just a beginner.
Farouq: And at the weekends – what do you do?
Peter: Well, on Friday mornings I go to the supermarket and after that I have my driving lesson. Then in the afternoon I usually visit some of my friends.
Farouq: And do you rest on Saturdays?
Peter: Not really. I always get up early and go to the beach and after lunch I play tennis. And then later in the evening I prepare my classes.
Farouq: You have a busy week!

a How many classes does Peter teach?
b Does he teach in the evenings?
c Does he teach Arabic?
d When does Peter have his Arabic classes?
e When does he go to the supermarket?
f What does he do on Saturday mornings?

2 Write

Complete Peter's timetable. Write in: a) Arabic lesson, b) driving lesson, c) tennis, d) prepare classes, e) beach, f) supermarket

	Sunday	Monday	Tuesday	Wednesday	Thursday	Friday	Saturday
morning	←			teaching	→		
afternoon							
evening	←			teaching	→		

LOOK!

on
on Monday(s) **on** Wednesday(s) **on** Friday(s)
in the morning
but: on Friday morning

3 Write

Write in these words: **prepare**, **later**, **supermarket**, **stay**, **on**, **afternoon**

Sam: What do you do (a) __________ Thursday?
Ahmed: Not much. In the morning we go to the (b) __________. Then we go home and (c) __________ lunch.
Sam: And in the (d) __________?
Fatma: We usually (e) __________ at home and watch a video.
Ahmed: And we sometimes go for a walk (f) __________.

Write in these words: **always**, **about**, **then**, **every**, **phone**, **evening**, **busy**, **after**

Sam: Are you (g) __________ tomorrow morning, Salem?
Salem: Yes, I am. I go to the mosque (h) __________ Friday.
Sam: And (i) __________ that?
Salem: Well, I come home at (j) __________ two o'clock and (k) __________ we have lunch.
Sam: What about the (l) __________?
Salem: I'm sorry, Sam. We (m) __________ visit my wife's parents on Friday evenings.
Sam: Don't worry. I'll (n) __________ again on Saturday.

4 Ask and answer

Talk to another student.

A

What do you do at the weekends?

B

On Thursday ...	I	(always)	go to ...
On Friday ...		(usually)	stay at home.
On Saturday ...		(sometimes)	visit ...
On Sunday ...			watch ...

LOOK!

I usually go to the beach **Time**
on Fridays.
in the morning.
at eight o'clock.

Time
On Fridays I usually go to the beach.
In the morning
At eight o'clock

5 Listen and say

Say these words:

just, **jacket**, **jeans**, **job**, **jam**, **orange juice**, **Germany**, **George**, **engine**, **garage**

Now say these words:

go, **get**, **give**, **girl**, **guest**, **guard**, **big**, **bag**, **dog**, **glass**, **great**, **younger**

6 Listen and write

Put these words in the correct lists:

weekend, **get up**, **every**, **later**, **return**, **prepare**, **classes**, **because**

☐ ▫ weekend	▫ ☐ get up
__________	__________
__________	__________
__________	__________
__________	__________

LANGUAGE

on Friday
at the weekend
every
later
Verbs: to prepare, to visit

STUDY

When ...? What time ...?

When do you get up?
When do you start work?
(At) What time do you have breakfast?

always, usually, sometimes, never

I	**always**	get up early.
You	**usually**	go to the mosque on Fridays.
We	**sometimes**	start work at 8.
They		
He	**never**	gets up early.
She		goes to the mosque on Fridays.
		starts work at 8.

What's the time?

It's half past eight.
It's eight thirty.

It's a quarter past four.
It's four fifteen.

It's a quarter to eight.
It's seven forty-five.

on, in, at

on Friday(s)
on Friday afternoon(s)
in the morning/afternoon/evening
at night
at the weekend

every

every day/week/month/year
every Friday

Then/and then

Tom goes for a run. He has a shower.
Tom goes for a run **and then** he has a shower.
Tom goes for a run. **Then** he has a shower.

after/before

I have a rest **after** lunch.
I go for a walk **before** dinner.

NEW WORDS

Learn these words.

Food
yoghurt
cheese
eggs
olives
jam
honey

Meals
breakfast
lunch
dinner

Adjectives
early
hard
busy

Nouns
refinery
shower
college
weekend
rest
night shift
supermarket
class
lesson
quarter

Verbs
to walk
to leave
to rest
to run
to go for (a run)
to go for (a walk)
to get up
to get dressed
to prepare
to start
to stay
to visit
to return
to have (breakfast/a shower)
to pray

Write other new words here.

UNIT

6 On Holiday

Lesson 1 What's the weather like?

1 Match

It's ... **sunny**, **cloudy**, **windy**, **raining**.

______ ______ ______ ______

2 Listen and write

Write A, B, C or D.

A

What's the weather like, Mark?
It's hot and sunny.
Good. I'm going for a swim.
Me too.

B

Oh look!
What?
It's raining.
Raining? But it was sunny yesterday!
Well, it's raining now.

C

What's the weather like in the winter, Linda?
Terrible! It's very cold and windy.
Does it rain?
Yes. It usually rains in January and February.

D

Are you on holiday today, Waleed?
Yes, of course. It's National Day. Everyone's on holiday.
Let's go for a picnic.
Good idea. The weather's lovely.

3 Ask and answer

A		B	
What's the weather like?	It's	hot	(and ...)
		cold	
		sunny	
		cloudy	
		windy	
		raining	

LOOK!

Oh look! It's raining.
It usually rains in the winter.

LOOK!

yesterday
It **is** cold and windy **today**.
It **was** sunny **yesterday**.

4 Match

Match the questions with the answers.

1 What's Katherine like?

2 What's the weather like in the summer?

3 What's 'foul medames' like?

4 What's your uncle like?

5 What's Cairo like?

6 What're your children like?

7 What's your suitcase like?

a It's delicious.

b They're very clever.

c He's tall with black hair and a moustache.

d Terrible. It's very, very hot and sunny.

e It's black with a red handle.

f She's short and she's got brown hair and brown eyes.

g It's very big and noisy.

5 Write

Write in these words: **lovely**, **like**, **very**, **it's**, **terrible**, **raining**

A: What's the weather (a) ____________ in Toronto, Dad?

B: (b) ____________. It's (c) ____________ cold and it's (d) ____________.

A: Is it? It's (e) ____________ here. It's sunny and (f) ____________ not too hot.

B: You're lucky!

Write in these words: **weather**, **at**, **everyone**, **windy**, **quite**, **on**

C: How are you Sarah?

D: I'm fine thanks, Mum.

C: Are you (g) ____________ work?

D: No. Today's National Day. (h) ____________ is (i) ____________ holiday.

C: Is the (j) ____________ good?

D: Not bad. It's cold but (k) ____________ sunny.

C: It's very (l) ____________ here.

LOOK!

everyone

I am on holiday.

They are on holiday.

Everyone is on holiday.

Lesson 2 What are you doing?

1 Read

It's a holiday today. Hassan and his family are having a picnic at the National Park. It is a beautiful place with many trees and a lake. There is a small café too. The children are playing with some toys and Hassan's wife, Nadia, is preparing the lunch. A woman is taking a photograph of her friends. Some people are walking by the lake. Hassan is sleeping under a tree.

LAKESIDE CAFÉ
What are you doing Hassan?
I'm sleeping.

Write these words: preparing lunch, walking, playing, sleeping

a What is Hassan doing? He's ____________________

b What is Nadia doing? She's ____________________

c What are the children doing? They're ____________________

d What are some people doing? They're ____________________

LOOK!

-ing verbs

to be		**+ ... -ing**	
I am	We are	playing	going
You are	They are	sleeping	preparing
He/She/It is		doing	

2 Look and say

What are they doing?

He's ... -ing.
She's ....
They're ....

3 Write

Write these verbs in the **-ing** form. Write them in the correct lists.

walk, **prepare**, **swim**, **go**, **make**, **rain**, **run**, **play**, **drive**, **eat**, **take**, **get**

A sleeping, ______________________

B sitting, ______________________

C having, ______________________

LOOK!

Spelling

A	sleep		+	-ing	= sleeping
B	sit	+ t	+	-ing	= sitting
C	have	e̸	+	-ing	= having

4 Write

Today is a holiday. It's eleven o'clock in the morning. What is everyone doing? Put the verbs in the **-ing** form. For example:

Sam is visiting some friends. (visit)

a Amy ____________ lunch in the kitchen. (prepare)

b Tom and Mary ____________ to the beach. (drive)

c Gary ____________ a book in the garden. (read)

d Ahmed and his family ____________ in the park. (walk)

e Peter ____________ tennis with a friend. (play)

f Latifa and Sarah ____________ photographs. (take)

g Saeed is in his boat. He ____________. (fish)

h Mr Smith ____________ in the hotel. (work)

i Jamila and Mohsin are in the sitting room. They ____________ a video. (watch)

j Nick ____________ coffee in a café in the market. (have)

k Two boys ____________ in the lake. (swim)

l Wendy ____________ some coffee for her guests. (make)

LOOK!

What're you doing?
I'm waiting for a bus.

What're you doing?
We're waiting for a bus.

5 Write

What're you doing?

I ________ some fruit. (eat)

My sister and I ________ to the hospital. (go)

6 Listen and say

These words have the 'p' sound.

place, **people**, **play**, **pray**, **prepare**, **picnic**

LANGUAGE

Present Continuous Tense: to be + -ing

Verbs: to take (a photograph), to wait (for), to make, to sleep, to play, to think, to learn, to look at

under a tree
by the lake

Lesson 3 In a restaurant

1 **Listen and read**

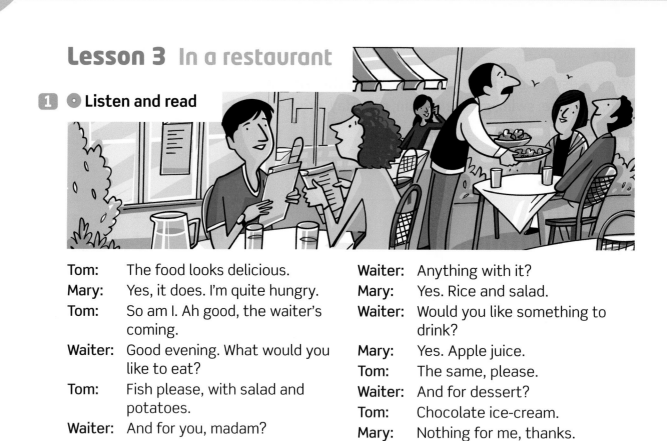

Tom:	The food looks delicious.
Mary:	Yes, it does. I'm quite hungry.
Tom:	So am I. Ah good, the waiter's coming.
Waiter:	Good evening. What would you like to eat?
Tom:	Fish please, with salad and potatoes.
Waiter:	And for you, madam?
Mary:	I'd like chicken.
Waiter:	Anything with it?
Mary:	Yes. Rice and salad.
Waiter:	Would you like something to drink?
Mary:	Yes. Apple juice.
Tom:	The same, please.
Waiter:	And for dessert?
Tom:	Chocolate ice-cream.
Mary:	Nothing for me, thanks.

What are they having for dinner? Tick (✓) the food and drink.

Tom

meat	☐	potatoes	☐
fish	☐	vegetables	☐
chicken	☐	fruit	☐
beefsteak	☐	yoghurt	☐
salad	☐	ice-cream	☐
rice	☐	apple juice	☐

Mary

meat	☐	potatoes	☐
fish	☐	vegetables	☐
chicken	☐	fruit	☐
beefsteak	☐	yoghurt	☐
salad	☐	ice-cream	☐
rice	☐	apple juice	☐

2 **Write**

What are Tom and Mary having for dinner?

a Tom is having _____.

b Mary _____.

3 **Listen and say**

☐☐☐ potatoes   ☐☐☐☐ vegetables   ☐ ☐☐ lamb kebab

☐ ☐ beefsteak   ☐ ☐ chocolate

What would you like to eat?
What would you like to drink?

LOOK!

desert/dessert

☐ ☐ desert

☐ ☐ dessert

4 Act it out

A You are the waiter. Ask:
What would you like to eat/to drink?
And for you?
Anything with it?
And for dessert?

B and **C** You are hungry and thirsty!
Choose five things from the menu. Say: I'd like...

Menu

soup	salad	**Drinks**
lamb kebab	bread	tea
chicken	**Dessert**	coffee
fish	ice-cream	Cola
beefsteak	fruit	apple juice
potatoes	cake	
rice		

5 Write

Write in these -ing verbs: **looking**, **having**, **sitting**, **standing**, **coming**, **waiting**, **saying**

LOOK!

something/anything/nothing
I'd like **something** to eat. I'm hungry.
Would you like **anything** with the chicken?
No, **nothing**, thank you.

Maryam and her husband are (a) __________ at a table in a coffee shop. They aren't very hungry and so they are just (b) __________ sandwiches. The coffee shop is very busy. Some people are (c) __________ at the door. They are (d) __________ for a table. The waiter is very slow. Maryam is (e) __________ at her watch. "Oh, good!" she is (f) __________ to her husband. "The waiter is (g) __________ with the sandwiches."

6 Listen and write

Sounds and spelling.

Write these words in the correct lists: **steak**, **head**, **read**, **friend**, **beef**, **police**, **red**, **take**, **eight**, **guest**, **people**, **wait**

steak	head	read
__________	__________	__________
__________	__________	__________
__________	__________	__________

LANGUAGE

What would you like to eat/to drink?
Food vocabulary
Verbs: to say, to stand, to eat, to drink

Lesson 4 Where are you going?

1 Listen

A

Where are you going, Liz?
I'm going to the supermarket.
Oh? Can I come with you?
Of course.

B

I'm sorry. I must go.
Are you going home?
No, I'm not. I'm going to the garage.
It closes at six o'clock.
OK. See you later, Mark.

C

Excuse me. Can I see your pass, please?
Sure. Here you are.
Where are you going?
To Mr Khalifa's office.
That's all right, Mr Smith. Please go in.

TAXI

D

Where are you going?
The airport. We're late.
OK. Get in.
How much is it?
Ten dinars.

Where are they going?

a Liz is going to ____________
b Mark's friend ____________
c Sam Smith ____________
d The two men ____________

LOOK!

Where are you going?	
Are you going home?	Yes, I am.
	No, I'm not.

2 Listen and say

Where are you going?
Are you going home?

3 Ask and answer

Ask four people:

Where are you going (after the lesson)?

	NAME	WHERE
1	____________	____________
2	____________	____________
3	____________	____________
4	____________	____________

4 Act it out

A You are a taxi driver. Ask:
Where are you going?
OK. Get in, please.
... pounds.

B You want a taxi to go to: the market/the airport/the bus station/the hospital
I'm going to ...
How much is it?
OK/That's too much!

LOOK!

go in/**get in**

go in

get in

5 Numbers

Match the numbers

ten, **fifty**, **a hundred**, **five hundred**, **a thousand**, **a hundred thousand**, **five hundred thousand**, **a million**

LOOK!

must
I must go. I'm late.
You must speak to the doctor.
He must study every evening.

100,000	100	1,000,000	1,000
1 ______	2 ______	3 ______	4 ______
500,000	10	50	500
5 ______	6 ______	7 ______	8 ______

6 Listen and say

These words all have "**th**":
thing, **something**, **think**, **nothing**, **three thirty**, **anything**, **bath**, **thin**

These words all have "**th**" too, but the sound is different:
then, **after that**, **with**, **weather**, **there**, **another**, **brother-in-law**, **the airport**

A: What's that?
B: What?
A: There. There's something in the bath.
B: In the bath? There's nothing.
A: There is.
B: Oh yes. That.
A: It's thin.
B: With long legs.
A: It's horrible!

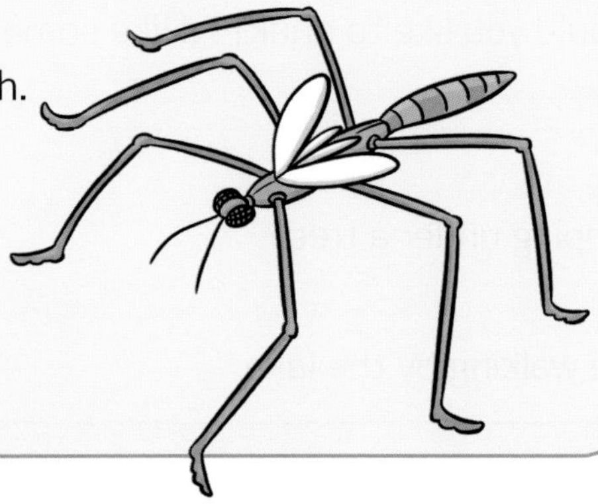

STUDY

The Present Continuous Tense

to be + -ing

I am	(not)	going	We are	(not)	going
You are		having	You are		having
He is		playing	They are		playing
She is		reading			reading
It is		sitting			sitting

What are you doing?	I'm having lunch.
Where are you going?	We're going to the market.
Are you going home?	Yes, I am./No, I'm not.

was/were

I was	We were
You were	You were
He was	They were
She was	
It was	

It was cold and windy yesterday.

must

I must go.
You must see a doctor.
He must study every evening.

something, anything, nothing

There's something in my soup.
Would you like anything to drink?
There's nothing in the fridge.
What would you like to eat? I'd like meat and rice.
What would you like to drink? I'd like some water.

under

He's sleeping under a tree.

by

They are walking by the lake.

NEW WORDS

Learn these words.

Adjectives
sunny
cloudy
windy
lovely
terrible
horrible

Food
soup
potatoes
vegetables
lamb
beef
beefsteak
kebab
chocolate

Verbs
to rain
to take (a photograph)
to wait (for)
to say
to stand
to get in
to make
to listen (to)
to sleep
to play
to think
to look at

Other
yesterday
the same
of course
see you later!
see you soon!
something
anything
nothing
everyone

Nouns
holiday
picnic
place
desert
dessert
toys
menu
lake
café

Write other new words here.

Revision C

Grammar

always/usually/sometimes/never

I		get up early.
You	always	
We	usually	
They	sometimes	
	never	
He	gets up early.	
She		
It		

LOOK!

I **sometimes** visit my aunt on Thursdays.
I don't **usually** work in the evening.
Do you **always** stay at home at the weekends?

1 Write

Put the words in the right order.

a afternoon / sometimes / in / rest / I / the

____

b on / never / Sam / Fridays / works /

____

c leaves / Nadia / at / thirty / office / always / two / her

____

d don't / to / they / school / morning /the / walk / usually / in

____

e picnic / for / in / summer / never / a / the / we /go

____

f in / watch / you / always / evenings / do / television / the / ?

____

g doesn't / the / Tunisia / summer / usually / it / in / rain / in

____

h have / Ahmed / does / canteen / the / in / always / breakfast / ?

____

2 Write

Write four sentences about your life with **always, usually**, **sometimes** and **never**.
For example: I always get up at six o'clock.

a ______________________________

b ______________________________

c ______________________________

d ______________________________

The Present Continuous Tense
to be + -ing
I am (not) watching
You are
He/She/It is
We are
You are
They are

3 What are they doing?

What are the people in the pictures doing? Write sentences.

a Noor

?

b Jane

c Lynn and Kate

d Keith and Scott

e Khalid

f Ann

SCHOOL

g ____________

h ____________

____

____

____

____

____

4 On the telephone

Put the verb in the Continuous form.

Sue: Hello, Samia. This is Sue.

Samia: Hello! How are you?

Sue: Fine. What (a) ____________ you ____________ (do)?

Samia: I (b) ____________ ____________ (prepare) lunch.

Sue: Oh.(c) ____________ you ____________ (cook) lamb?

Samia: No. We (d) ____________ ____________ (not have) a big lunch. Just a snack. Come and have lunch with us!

5 Write

Write **on**, **in** or **at**.

a I'll see you tomorrow ______________ ten o'clock.
You mean, ten o'clock ______________ the morning?
No, ten o'clock ______________ night.

b When were you born, Grandmother?
I was born ______________ 1910, ______________ June.

c Are you ______________ holiday this week?
No. We never have our holidays ______________ the winter.

d Are you busy ______________ the weekend?
I'm busy ______________ Thursday. But I'm free ______________ Friday afternoon.

e Where's Saeed. Is he ______________ work?
I think he's ______________ home ______________ the moment.

6 Question words

Match the questions with the answers.

a when does the class start?
b Which company do you work for?
c Why do you always drive to my house? It's not far.
d Who is that man?
e Where do you come from?
f What's that under the cupboard?
g Whose jacket is this?
h How is the soup?
i How much is this?
j How many days are there in this month?

1 It's the cat.
2 Soon.
3 Five pounds.
4 Tom's.
5 Middle East Trading.
6 Algeria.
7 Because I'm lazy!
8 I'm not sure.
9 Mark.
10 Fantastic!

NEW WORDS

7 Verbs

Match the verbs with the noun.

Verb

get in, make, listen to, wait for, go for, cook, return, start

Noun

work, tea, the radio, lunch, home, a walk, the car, a bus

8 Food

Match the words with the pictures.
kebab, vegetables, honey, salad, rice, chocolate, potatoes, soup

1 ____________

2 ____________

3 ____________

4 ____________

5 ____________

6 ____________

7 ____________

8 ____________

9 Write

Write these words in the sentences: **desert**, **beef**, **weather**, **menu**, **dinner**, **toy**, **lake**, **same**, **lamb**, **refinery**, **lesson**

a The baby is playing with a new ____________.

b Ahmed works in an oil ____________.

c What time does the English ____________ start?

d ____________ and ____________ are both meat.

e I'm having apple pie. Would you like the ____________?

f We always have picnics in the ____________ in the winter.

g I never swim in that ____________. The water is dirty.

h Can I see the ____________ please? We want something to eat.

i The ____________ is terrible today. Let's stay home.

j We usually have ____________ at about seven o'clock in the evening.

10 Look and say

What's the time?

It's ... o'clock.
It's half past ...
It's a quarter past/to ...
It's ... thirty/fifteen.

a 

b 

c 
6:45

d 

e 

f 
12:15

g 

h 

i 

j 

Punctuation

11 Write

Write the sentences with punctuation and capital letters.

a i live in king john street

b jawad goes to manama boys secondary school

c theyre having lunch in the momtaz restaurant

d keith and scott aren't going to doha today

e its about seven oclock

f tomorrow is national day in oman

g were going to the national park for a picnic

h sara doesnt study science she studies mathematics

i mr and mrs brown dont speak arabic very well

j we usually go to al alpha supermarket on thursdays

k thats marks bag give it to him

l it isnt raining now lets go out

Spelling

12 Look

There are two spelling mistakes in every line.

a A: *Can I speek to Mr Parker, pleas?*
b B: *I'm sarry. Mr Parker's busy. He's teeching.*
c A: *At what time dose the leson finish?*
d B: *It finishs at about twelve tharty.*
e A: *I'll phone agin aftre the lesson.*

Pronunciation

13 Match

Match the words that have the same sounds.

now steak seat soup fish get course night eight trousers sit head beef horse like too

Read and Write

14 Read

Read about Latifa's holiday.

Al Quds Hotel
King Hussein Street
Amman
Jordan
12 June 2011

Dear Sarah,
Hello. How are you? I hope you are well.
I'm enjoying my holiday here in Jordan with my brother and my sister. We're staying at the Al Quds Hotel which is quite good and not very expensive. At the moment I am sitting in the hotel with my, brother and writing this letter to you. The weather is very hot here in Amman and I am drinking cold fruit juice!
We were in the market this morning and it was very busy and very noisy.
We go to the market every morning. My sister loves shopping! She's got a lot of new dresses. In the evening we usually visit my cousin, Muna. She's a student at the university here. She lives in a district of Amman called Shmeisani. It's quite a long way and so we take a taxi. This afternoon we're going to a museum not far from the hotel. Yesterday we went to a restaurant with my cousin. The food was terrible and so I don't feel very well this morning!
Tomorrow we are going to Damascus for a few days. I have another cousin in Damascus. His name's Ali and he works in the embassy. After that we will return to Amman and then fly back to Muscat.
See you soon.
Best wishes,
Latifa

a Which city is Latifa in?
b Where is Latifa going tomorrow?
c What is Latifa doing at the moment?
d What is the weather like?
e Where do they usually go in the evenings?
f Where are they going this afternoon?
g Where does Ali live?

15 Write

Join these sentences with **and then**. For example:

Tom has breakfast. He drives to work.

Tom has breakfast and then he drives to work.

a Waleed has lunch at two o'clock. He goes to the club.

____

b The English class finishes at four thirty. I drive home.

____

c On Wednesday Amy finishes work early. She visits her aunt in the hospital.

____

d It usually rains in the morning. It is sunny in the afternoon.

____

e We usually have a big lunch. We don't eat very much in the evening.

____

f Rashid usually studies for two hours after dinner. He goes to bed.

____

g You always look at my answers. You write them in your book!

____

16 Write

Write about the people in this picture. Use the verbs: **sit**, **have**, **look**, **drink**, **swim**, **walk**, **talk**, **listen**, **drive**

Begin: 'Some people are having a picnic on the beach.'

Story: Hello London 6

Ali and his grandfather are at the end of their holiday in London. They are returning to Dubai tomorrow.

1
Hello, Ali. What are you doing?
Nothing much. I'm reading a newspaper ...
2
... and grandfather is getting dressed.
3
I'm going to Brighton. Would you and your grandfather like to come?
OK. But where's Brighton?
4
It's not far from London. It's by the sea.
Two hours later they are in Brighton.
5
Well, this is Brighton. Do you like it?
It's a nice place, but it's cold isn't it?
6
Yes, it is now. We usually come here in the summer. The weather's good then.
7
We always stay in this hotel.
BLUE SEA HOTEL
8
FISH + CHIPS
I'm taking a photograph. Smile please!
9
Would you like something to drink, David?
seaside cafe
Yes, good idea. I'd like some coffee.
10
It's late. I think we must go soon.
Yes. We're going home tomorrow morning.
At the airport.
11
Well, goodbye. Have a good trip.
Thank you very much. We hope to see you all in Dubai.
I hope so.
12

Notes

Notes

Notes

Notes

Notes

Notes

Notes

Notes

Pearson Limited
Edinburgh Gate
Harlow
Essex CM20 2JE
England
and Associated Companies throughout the World

www.pearsonlongman.com

First published 2011

20 19 18 17 16 15 14

IMP 10 9 8 7 6 5 4 3

ISBN: 9781408285732

Illustrations by: Adrian Barclay, Richard Jones and Matt Ward, Beehive Illustration Ltd

The publisher would like to thank the following for their kind permission to reproduce their photographs:

(Key: b-bottom; c-centre; l-left; r-right; t-top)

Alamy Images: Bon Appetit 16br, Brand X 16bc (chicken), Caro 11tl, David Young-Wolff 71bl, foodfolio 16bc, Hypermania 6br, ICP-Traffic 11c, imagebroker 9cl, 56r, IMAGEMORE Co.Ltd 9cr, 56c, minden mas 11cr, Mode Images Limited 9c (baseball cap), Neil Fraser 5tr, Niall McDiarmid 45cl, 56tr, Oleksiy Maksymenko 5bc, 45c (suit), 56bl, Petru Emanuel Vasiu 39tc, 39tr, Petru Emanuel Vasiu 39tc, 39tr, PhotoStock 14bl, Pick and Mix Images 56br, SoFood 62l, Squint 6bl, 27c (letter), stu49 5cr, Tim Hill 14br, TNT Magazine 5tl, Valeriya Potapova 5c, Viktor Fischer 16bc (rice); Comstock Images: 14bc (sandwich); Fotolia.com: 27cl; iStockphoto: 5tc, 5cl, 5br, 6bc (back of envelope), 6bc (letter), 9c (sailor's cap), 11tr, 27cl (envelope), 27cr (computer), 39tl, 39c, 39cl, 39cr, 45c, 45cr, 45bc (cap), 45bc (t shirt), 45br, 56tc (sailor's cap), 56tc (trousers), 56bc (red cap), 56bc (shirt), 62r, 83tl, 83tr, 83cl, 83cr, 83bc (rice), 83bc (vegetables), 83br; Photolibrary.com: 15tc, 16bl, 62cl, 81br, 83bl, Pixtal 71tl; PunchStock: 5r (camera); Shutterstock.com: 5bl, 45tc, 56tl

Cover images: Front: Alamy Images: Robert Adrian Hillman

Every effort has been made to trace the copyright holders and we apologise in advance for any unintentional omissions. We would be pleased to insert the appropriate acknowledgement in any subsequent edition of this publication.

Prepared for publication by Clare Webber

Printed in Slovakia by Neografia